CHRISTIAN DE

CW00555743

BOOK 2

"Engaging The Enemy"

SWORD PUBLICATIONS Ltd
Summerhill Court
Lang Stracht
Aberdeen AB2 6TT U.K.
Telephone (01224) 326622

PART TWO OF A TEACHING
MANUAL ON CASTING OUT DEMONS
FOR CHRISTAN SOLDIERS

PETER HOBSON

Quotations from the New Testament are generally my own translation, otherwise I have usually used The Revised Standard Version of the Bible.

1st Edition 1986
2nd Edition 1993

National Library of Australia I.S.B.N.
Christian Deliverance Series 0 947252 00 2 (set)
Book 2 "Engaging the Enemy" 0 947252 02 9

Printed in Sri Lanka

To my "new" wife of 35 years
of marriage, Verlie, made new
by the delivering and restoring
grace of the Lord Jesus, and
now herself a front-line soldier
in His deliverance ministry.

CHRISTIAN DELIVERANCE

PREFACE TO BOOK 2

"ENGAGING THE ENEMY"

This series has been written in order to provide Christian soldiers with both revelational material and very practical "hands-on" guidance in all matters relating to the effective exercise of the Deliverance Ministry of Christ Jesus.

Nothing contained herein should be interpreted as impinging on or sharing in the glory that alone belongs to the Godhead; Father, Son and Holy Spirit, because nothing we attempt in His Name can succeed without His Presence and His grace—praise His Holy Name!

On the other hand I am persuaded that no genuine disciple and soldier of Christ should fail to be the involved, victorious warrior He has authorised, called and chosen us to be. Let us cease to say "If God wants to do it, He will do it", when He has plainly commanded and commissioned His Church to act in His Name.

May our words be His words. May our hand be His Hand, and feet His feet . May our eyes and ears be His eyes and ears, and our hearts His heart.

This book is not about theological theories, although there should be enough theology in it to satisfy most serious students.

It is about getting the job done—by His grace and command!

I have tried to arrange the teaching material of this series of deliverance manuals in such a way that I could add truth to truth, step by step and not shock suddenly or offend un-necessarily. It follows that you may find Book 2 a revelational progression from Book I and I hope it will whet your spiritual appetite even more for Books 3 and 4. If you can stay with me all the way to the end of Book 4 (notwithstanding a few question marks in your mind, which is to be expected), I am sure that you will be a vastly better informed Christian about spiritual warfare.

Wishing you every rich blessing in Christ Jesus.

Peter Hobson
SYDNEY, NSW.
March, 1986.

CONTENTS

BOOK 2 "ENGAGING THE ENEMY"

INTRODUCTION

This is Book 2 in the series on Christian Deliverance, and the Index of the proposed Book 3 can be found at rear under Appendix H. I hope you will take the trouble to obtain and read the whole series in order to have a rounded picture of the dynamic relevance and operation of Christ's deliverance ministry for the Body of Christ TODAY!

Rarely have books been written, checked, typed, etc., to final presentation under such great difficulties. I have personally received quite a lot of deliverance during this preparatory work, begun thirteen years ago - Praise the Lord - as spirits of mind control, confusion and fatigue sought to overtake me and block my clarity, memory recall and the spiritual revelation of the Word of God.

I have often picked up the typescript to work and ended up under the power of God and getting deliverance. Indeed it has been battle, battle, all the way, but I have also been immeasurably blessed by all the victories. Those who have assisted me with typing have shared in these battles also.

The early pages of this book are taken up with methodology. which is an area where there is little biblical information to go on. If you are not immediately interested in the potential of group or mass deliverance for your ministry or assembly in the near future, please bear with this very practical material. It will repay careful study.

As the material in this series expands more and more in the production process, I have been obliged to add a fourth book with a view to expanding discussion on the impact of the ministry, and detailing a wide range of areas where the Lord has given revelational discernment for the benefit of the Body of Christ. I propose to make special reference to the permeation of religious spirits masquerading as the Holy Spirit throughout the Church, in both Born Again and un-saved church goers, especially the former.

I was interested to read a comment by **Professor Peter Wagner** of Fuller Theological Seminary, Pasadena, California. In answer to the question "What do you think about the ministries of deliverance or exorcism?" he said -

> "I think that we haven't even begun to tap the resources that we have in the ministries of deliverance. I think we haven't begun to recognize the actual direct power of evil in our lives. I am beginning to wonder if we've been playing games, particularly talking about Christian social action or political action or overthrowing governments. The way I am beginning to see it is that those kind of approaches may be trivial because we battle against the principalities and powers, and those aren't the presidents and dictators of the world; those are the demonic forces. **If we don't learn how to confront these demonic forces directly in a spiritual battle, I think we are playing games.**"
> Restore Magazine - March, 1985.

It seems that the message of the Holy Spirit is coming through louder and clearer that the Church of God HAS BEEN PLAYING GAMES, theological and intellectual games while the people of God, and indeed the people of the world, have been torn to pieces by ruthless and merciless spiritual wolves. But - thank the Lord - **flesh and blood does not bring revelations such as that to men like Peter Wagner, but our Heavenly Father,** and what He has shown Professor Wagner, He is showing to others also. The time of awakening is here!

As we now go into the battle arena to actually engage the enemy, let us quickly refresh ourselves with the subject headings of what we have learnt when making ourselves ready in Book 1:-

CHAPTER 1 UNDERSTANDING THE PROBLEM

1.	Clarifying of Terms

CHAPTER 4   PREPARATION OF THE SUFFERER

1.   Initial Contact

   (i) Sorting out enquiries
   (ii) Church allegiance

2   The Interview

   (i)   Length of interviews
   (ii) Putting them at ease
   (iii) Gathering personal information
   (iv) Trust only the Holy Spirit
   (v)   A second witness
   (vi) Security of personal information
   (vii) What to reveal

3.   Trust, Submission and Co-operation

   (i) Fellowship and Teaching

4.   Permission to Minister

   (i)   Overcoming a change of heart/mind
   (ii) A possible solution to avoid slander
   (iii) Hatred

Personal Note from the Author

APPENDICES

A.   The Bible's Condemnation of the Occult
B.   "So You Think You Need Deliverance?"
C.   "Permission to Minister" authority — Book 1
D.   Bible Notes on Demonology
E.   Breaking Curses

CHAPTER 5

THE HEART OF THE MINISTRY

5.1   PRACTICAL CONSIDERATIONS.

INTRODUCTION

How can the "average" Pastor get started in Deliverance ministry? Well, I think that, for many of you, the Lord will start you off the same way He did with us - except that you may not need to learn as slowly as we did because, if you are wise, you won't get into a position where the Lord has to force you into changes as a matter of economy of time, as was the case with us. You will learn quickly what we learnt slowly over many years.

Some will probably begin by finding that a Christian for whom you are praying for healing **is not responding** and you will become convicted by the Holy Spirit that a causal demon is resisting the healing ministry. At that point you either wring your hands in despair and pull back out of the conflict, or you take up the challenge in Jesus' Name

One becomes two

You start with one here, and one there. You draw in spiritual support - counsellors, witnesses - people you can trust; people with faith and courage and who REALLY believe that they "can do all things (commissioned in the Word) through Christ who strengthens them." One sufferer becomes two, and then three, and all the time Christ is teaching, guiding and encouraging so that, like the early disciples under the exhilaration of the Holy Spirit, you can rejoice before the Lord and say, **"Even the demons are subject to us in your Name!"** (Luke 10:17). As with the early disciples, it will be necessary for the Lord to **curb your enthusiasm** due to easy initial victories lest it become a snare for you. You will meet apparent defeat from time to time in order that you may realise your total dependance upon the

Presence, the anointing, of the Lord Jesus - that you are nothing without Him; you do not have ALL discernment and you do not have ALL faith so as to remove mountains - yet!

The Lord will train you, step by step.

You begin where the need is, and move ahead WITH the Lord. You don't rush ahead and you don't lag too far behind, but seek to move WITH Him; and as the Spirit leads, let your people know that Christ is TRULY SUFFICIENT for ALL their needs and YOU are prepared to put your belief into ACTION, not just talk. Talk is cheap, and the Kingdom of God is not about talk but POWER (1 Cor 4:20).

How can this be accomplished for YOUR assembly?

(i) SINGLE OR GROUP MINISTRY?

T.L. Osborn's Revelation

Twenty six years ago I read "Healing En Masse" by a man who is arguably the greatest Christian evangelist of all time - T.L. Osborn. In this book he shares how during crusades in Flint, Michigan (U.S.A.) and Ponce (Puerto Rico) the Lord answered a great need.

Brother Osborn had exhausted himself earlier in Jamaica, where, night after night, he "prayed for the sick one by one, ministering to seemingly endless lines of sufferers."

He goes on to say:

> *"As I stood on the platform in Flint, something happened to me; like a light from heaven the truths of mass healing suddenly shined into my soul.*
>
> *God seemed to say to me 'Why do you limit my power? I can heal ten thousand as easily as one...'*

Then I thought: Since I can pray and God hears and answers my prayer, why do I not ask God to perform a thousand miracles at the same time? If He is God, His power is unlimited! If He can do one miracle, He can do a thousand miracles at the same time! Why not ask Him to heal EVERYONE who is sick at the same time?

As Jonathan said to his armour-bearer, 'There is no restraint to the Lord to save by MANY or by FEW' (1 Sam. 14:6)....

I knew that if a thousand people wanted to accept Christ and be saved, I would not pray for each one individually; I would teach them all to call on the Lord and to believe at one time. All who believed would be saved.

I knew the same method should be followed in ministering to the sick.

I should not confine God's healing power to the limits of my own strength and leave the rest of the people to wait until the next night to be healed. Some of them might die before their turn would come. I knew it was God's will to heal EVERYONE of them at once.

Standing there on the platform in Flint, Michigan, these things were going through my mind.

I made a decision to act on what God was showing me.

I called for every person in the audience who was totally deaf in one or both ears to come forward.

Fifty-four persons responded.

As I stood looking at those 54 persons I knew Christ

had given me 'power and authority over ALL devils, and to cure diseases' (Luke 9:1).

There were 54 deaf spirits at least. If I had 'power and authority over ALL devils' then I could cast ALL 54 of them out at one time as easy as one.

I prayed earnestly. I commanded every spirit of deafness to leave the people at once.

All of those present received their hearing immediately, except three. By the next day, they too had recovered.

I knew that **mass prayer, mass faith, mass healing**[1] was the answer to demonstrating the Gospel on a mass evangelistic scale...!

So it was that in Ponce, Puerto Rico I was practically forced to resort to mass prayer - to HEALING EN MASSE.

It was either HEALING EN MASSE or limit the scope of the campaign and of God's healing power. I chose to step aside and let God through to the people unhindered by my human limitations.

Day after day I instructed the multitudes in individual faith, urging every person to do his own asking, his own believing and his own receiving.

I taught the people to know their own rights in Christ, to claim what belonged to them individually, to act their own faith and to receive the answers to their own prayers.

---

1   To which I would add "mass deliverance" as well.

Instead of a few being blessed, thousands were healed every day".[1]

When I read these words twenty six years ago they made such an impression on me I knew in my spirit that one day I would put them to good use, by the grace of God.

As I was revising this book for its second edition, one of my deacons brought to my attention that **Rev. Don Basham,** who wrote **"Deliver Us From Evil"** and, along with **Derek Prince,** is a genuine pioneer of the re-discovery of deliverance for today, began **group deliverance ministry** in America, some time before 1972.

He writes:

"Alice and I were trying to spend a quiet evening at home when, as on many another evening, we were interrupted. A family seeking deliverance for their thirteen-year-old daughter. A spirit of asthma identified itself and spoke through the girl's own lips.

'I won't come out,' it snarled. 'This girl belongs to me!' Then, as I commanded the spirit to leave, the girl's eleven-year-old brother who had been sitting across the room suddenly began to gasp. 'No! No!' a whiny voice spoke out of him. 'I won't come out either!'

I turned to the parents, astonished. Yes, they said, the boy, too, had a lifelong history of breathing problems, though not so severe as his sister's. At length both children went through the typical contortions of an asthmatic attack, followed by sudden happy relief. Identical spirits of asthma left sister and brother simultaneously! As the significance of what I had seen began to sink in, my heart began to thump. If two people could be delivered by a single command, why not ten? Twenty?"

---

1   "Healing En Masse" pages 11–17

Don then goes on to describe his learning experience regarding when and how to minister to groups, especially when requested as a VISITING minister. He adds:

"So I came to see that there were three essential factors involved in the presentation of group deliverance. (1) Recognition of the needs for this ministry by the recognized spiritual leadership in a given area before the invitation to an "outside authority" goes out. (2) Clear scriptural teaching on the ministry followed by demonstration. (3) Careful follow-up by local leaders, setting deliverance into total spiritual ministry available to Christians in that place". (Pages 195 – 196)

When I was first led into this ministry I felt that everyone should be ministered to privately, and as people came from far and wide, I found that deliverance ministry was consuming as much as six hours prime time a day. As there are many other obligations on a Parish minister, and being convicted NOT to turn people away I found myself putting two and three people together for a ministry session. **We eventually progressed to having one ministry session per day** to which a manageable number of people would come.

As this was still emotionally and spiritually exhausting in the contest of busy Parish life, with school Scripture lessons to prepare and give, hospital and general visiting, counselling, sermon preparation etc., **we ended up with two large groups a week,** Sunday afternoon and mid-week.

Output and input

The point of what I am saying is that this "system" evolved purely from the enormous pressures of TIME and our own **physical, spiritual and emotional output.** We had to make time for God to minister His Spirit TO US (the team of counsellors).**There had to be an INPUT of the Holy Spirit** from above, a time and place for strengthening of our SPIRIT, soul and body to face the fresh challenges coming constantly to us. Otherwise how could we hope to cope, in our own strength, with everything expected of us? And, of course, T.L. Osborn's revelation encouraged me greatly.

Today, some twenty (20) years later, without traditional church or Parish duties, we plan only **ONE deliverance and healing[1] meeting per week,** as well as our normal Sunday Worship, and allow for emergency ministry and counselling during the week. I think it true to say that the effectiveness of my wife and I as deliverance ministers has increased enormously - praise the Lord - since those early days, and we could not have done then what we are doing now in 1993. The ministry has evolved under the guidance of the Holy Spirit and He has increased the Power and Anointing available to us, that we might be able to handle the increased warfare.

At this point you may ask the question, **"Why is Peter talking about Group Ministry** in this important chapter 'The Heart of the Ministry'? I'm not interested in that kind of volume work; I just want to help the odd person (no pun intended) in need in our assembly".

That is what I thought too, at the beginning, because I thought that the ministry today had the same impetus and objectives that Jesus' ministry had nineteen centuries ago.

"Different from N.T. times

But there is a big difference. Jesus ministered deliverance and healing then as a demonstration of His compassion, power, and the Kingdom of God which He preached. It was a ministry to **generally visible, external problems** of an obvious nature - things which stood out as the works of the devil. Today the Lord is **preparing His people with an inner cleansing** from the problems which exist deep within the inner person, where they are not so obvious. Indeed it is the hidden problems not

---

1   Now called Deliverance and Restoration (D. and R.)

obvious to men but seen by God alone that the Holy Spirit is searching out today, that the Bride of Christ might be truly without spot or blemish when the Bridegroom comes for her. THIS is the Great Salvation ready to be revealed in the last time (1 Peter 1:5) and **there will be only ONE GENERATION of the Bride (church) so cleansed** - the generation that is caught up in the air to meet the Lord! (1 Thess. 4:17) She will not only be "without spot or wrinkle" to look at (Eph. 5:27) but also "all glorious within" (Ps. 45:13 KJV). This is her high calling from God, her goal, her aim. God's purposes for the ministry have not changed since Jesus' earthly walk but now they are more urgent, more far-reaching, and more openly revealed in God's Plan of the Ages (Col. 1:25-27). **Today there is a different thrust, a vital thrust,** so that the Plan of the Ages should be fulfilled - and it will be fulfilled, possibly during what remains of this 20th century, or soon after.

Therefore the ministry of Jesus' healing and deliverance is now being expanded. It is not only to **external** needs but also to **internal** needs. It is not only to the **obvious** but to the **hidden;** it is not only to the **isolated** person in need, here and there - it is to **all** who belong to the Bride. It is no longer **particular,** but **total.** It is no longer an **option,** as some have thought, but it is a **command,** for the Lord has commanded, **"Be ye Holy even as I am Holy!"** (1 Peter 1:16) **You, therefore, must be perfect even as your Heavenly Father is perfect** (Matt. 5:48); **cleanse yourselves from every defilement of flesh and spirit** (2 Cor. 7:1); **be** (truly and fully) **filled with the Spirit** (Eph. 5:18). Even as John the Baptist preached before the first coming of the Lord, **"Prepare the way of the Lord, make His paths straight,"** so today also we must make ourselves ready (Luke 3:4-9) for the axe of God has truly been laid to the root of the trees and judgement begins-indeed, has already begun-with the people of God (1 Peter 4:17). The cry goes up again to the people of God—REPENT! MAKE YOURSELVES READY for the Bridegroom![1] This is not to bring an unclean

---

1   This Vision for the End - Time is expaded more fully in "End - Time Deliverance."

guilt and condemnation upon the church, but it is for her cleansing. Repentance breaks stiff-necked arrogance and haughtiness, defeats self-justification and pathetic excuses that constitute self-deception. Repentance enables us to truly forgive others who have sinned against us and also, through forgiveness of our own sins, repentance reconciles us totally to our Heavenly Father without any wall of remaining sin between us and Him.

Steps to begin

Let us assume that you have counselled a number of people in your church and, because time is so precious, you realise that you can't possibly minister to them one at a time or you would never get anything else done; especially if many will need continuing ministry for several weeks, even months, on the one kind of spiritual kingdom-and then who knows what the Holy Spirit may turn up next?

You only have one voice and perhaps 16 working hours a day with which to serve the Lord, but looking at your congregation, your flock over whom Christ has made you an under-shepherd, you realise the widespread need for deliverance amongst them.

The wolves somehow have got in amongst them and you have no desire to be cast in the role of a hireling who leaves the sheep at the mercy of ravenous wolves and flees. You care for sheep - you are not a Christian leader who does his job for hire and doesn't care. As Christ laid down His life for the sheep (even you), so you too have given your life in the service of Christ's sheep (John 10:11–18).

So you are faced with the enormous needs of your flock and a limited number of hours in the week; and **you accept the need to begin a continuous Deliverance and Healing group ministry** because you appreciate that there is no other way the church and every "living stone" that makes up the church can be cleansed in time to be part of the beautiful Bride for which the Lord is returning.

The ministry today is for all who are in the Body of Christ, and God's Plan will only be achieved by repentance throughout the world-wide church. What a shaking is going to take place - and what a Great Salvation is going to be revealed! Hallelujah!

So, why not ask yourself (as you read this book), what is YOUR part in these earth-shaking purposes of God?

(ii) PLANNING THE DELIVERANCE MEETING

Let us look at some **suggested methods for group ministry,** as this would be more complex in operation than individual treatment. These suggestions can always be TAILORED DOWN AND SIMPLIFIED FOR "SINGLE SUBJECT" DELIVERANCE ACCORDING TO EACH AND EVERY SITUATION.

The Deliverance ministry of Christ is not something people normally relish for themselves. They usually try every other avenue or solution in order to solve their emotional and/or mental problems, but finally - when nothing else works - some Christians, perhaps braver than the others (or perhaps more desperate), finally yield themselves into the hands of a Christian deliverance minister, because they think that what they are going to go through cannot be as bad as what they have been going through.

However, a great many (perhaps representing a very large percentage of all Christians) **prefer to put up with their bondages** because they are not quite desperate enough and view the medicine of "exorcism," as it is unfortunately often called, as probably worse than the infirmity they bear, and consequently do nothing effective, but continue in their bondages, vainly hoping that praise or something else will work the required miracle.

Perhaps your assembly has a number of those Christians who

know deep down in their spirit they need the ministry of deliverance, but the thought of private sessions during the week, with lots of yelling (by the minister), possible screaming and other manifestations (from themselves - ugh!), the noise, fear of humiliation and potential ugliness, all seems just too much to handle - even to think about - especially as some sessions can go on for hours, with everybody ending up exhausted spiritually, emotionally and physically; and the prospect of having to receive ministry over a series of such sessions is not very inviting. **With this kind of deliverance set-up, the medicine can seem worse than the affliction!**

However, praise God,

I want to say now, LOUDLY and CLEARLY, that for nine out of ten people, deliverance doesn't have to be like that. Let me say that again -

IT DOESN'T HAVE TO BE LIKE THAT!

Needful people can get deliverance as the Spirit moves sovereignly through a congregation --

-- AS THEY PRAISE AND WORSHIP the Lord

-- AS THEY LISTEN to Bible messages

-- and AS THEY PRAY --

all in fellowship with other Christians.

If you say, "Hey, that sounds great!" - then let me tell you more good news. That is how we (in Full Salvation Fellowship) believe that the Lord wants EVERY faithful fellowship to operate in this last hour. That is the way He has taught us and that is what we are sharing with Christian leaders who have ears to hear, hearts of shepherd's love, and the faith to act.

Simple – easier – time effective

Not only is this method easier and more simple for both subject and minister alike, but it is the only way the massive clean-up work of God can take place *in the time available.*

This method and principle of combined ministry can be used for any form of group deliverance, whether it be:

> **(a) normal public assemblies (church meetings)**
>
> **(b) private group (small - by invitation only), or**
>
> **(c) a Deliverance and Restoration (D. and R.) continuous ministry program, to which all Christians can be invited.**

(a) NORMAL CHURCH

I would like to treat EVERY NORMAL ASSEMBLY (WORSHIP MEETING) as an opportunity for the ministry of deliverance.

Many Christians believe (in theory) that the church meeting is the place for the exercise of all the other spiritual gifts so why should we not follow the scriptural principle that Jesus will exercise His Lordship over His people whenever they have gathered in His Name; and minister to their needs through ALL the gifts He has given to His Body? Why not deliverance? Yes, in normal church services or meetings?

Through sheer pressure of time (and it can be so time-consuming) and weight of experience, we have been taught of the Lord a new concept in deliverance where whole congregations can receive ministry in the course of normal worship and praise meetings; and where, as the Spirit moves over the whole assembly touching this one here and that one there according to His sovereignty, He leads the deliverance minister(s) and gives a word of knowledge and discernment of spirits etc. wherever necessary.

We have already discussed in Book 1, Chapter 2, the various possible ministries which can effect deliverance such as worship, the preached Word etc. and suggested that all these ministries flowing in the Body of Christ, with the love and presence of Jesus in the Body, make an anointed context for a powerful application of deliverance.

And this is exactly what we do have when a church congregation which is moving in the things of the Holy Spirit gathers to worship and praise the Lord, and to hear His Holy Word - both from the Holy Scriptures and from prophets in the Body. We HAVE the PRESENCE of JESUS! **What better context in which to minister deliverance?** Jesus is there! He is YAHWEH - SHAMMAH (The LORD is there - Ezek. 48:35).

So how would we exercise the ministry of deliverance in the middle of a church assembly? Well, at least two methods are possible:

(i) INVITATION AT THE END OF A MEETING

Let us consider deliverance ministry at the end of a meeting first, because this is fairly common in Renewal services today.

The minister can, in his appeal for enquirers to come to the Cross of Jesus and yield up their lives to Him, also include an invitation to those who need healing and/or deliverance to come forward for the appropriate ministry by those who are appointed to minister deliverance. Under this type of format, the ministering of a full salvation (i.e. evangelism, healing and deliverance) would normally occur towards the close of a meeting, which could then **be greatly prolonged,** and experience **flow-on problems** for **both those involved** in deliverance battles, and **others not involved**, who simply want some informal fellowship with other brethren before going home.

(ii) INVITATION AT THE BEGINNING

A second method, which requires a little courage, but would really open up your meetings to the leading and power of the Holy Spirit, would be to exercise your authority over any powers of darkness present in the meeting (in the people) - out loud - **at the very beginning of the meeting:** after appropriate opening prayers.

It is true that SOME deliverance takes place in most worship services where the meeting is being led by the Holy Spirit - probably more than the Pastor will ever realise this side of Heaven, but it is also true that such a small stream of deliverance can be turned into a veritable torrent - in which even rulers and authorities would have to bow the knee and depart. How do we turn the stream into a torrent? Simply by including deliverance prayers and commands **at the opening of the service. Ask, believe and act!**

This would mean that throughout the worship and praise, the preaching etc., unclean spirits would continue to leave the people of God in the meeting, until binding instructions were issued before the close. (Details of prayers, commands and instructions to demons will be discussed very shortly).

It would mean that at any time during the service[1] a wail or a shriek could burst out. Some could drop to the floor under the power of God, but if you have given over the meeting to the Lordship of Christ and the people of God are sensitive to the Spirit, and everyone knows and is rejoicing in the victories being won, then the anointing and presence of Christ will be so heavy upon the meeting that you will want the meeting and the blessing to go on forever (Matt. 12:28).

The beauty of this method is that the Lord is working His gracious, invisible work throughout the whole length of the

---

1   We have audio cassette tapes of our meetings available to Pastors and other accredited leaders on request.

meeting, deliverance is continuous rather than brief, and any **unbelievers in your church will come under tremendous conviction** - the kind of conviction that will either bring them to the Cross or take them out through the church doors. In such a meeting it will be impossible for anyone to remain "neutral."

In other words, you can get your deliverance during your normal weekly worship at the same time as many others around you, and no extra hours of private ministry are required.

I look forward to the day when EVERY true Christian assembly and meeting has the delivering and healing power of God moving continuously through it from beginning to end. I believe this will eventually come to pass amongst the churches of the five wise virgins, but sad to say, the "foolish virgin" churches will scoff and please themselves, for they will not sense the time of visitation of the Lord, being deaf to the cry of the prophets of God in this age, and blind to their own spiritual poverty.

The problems associated with this method of using the assembly as a large "group" are basically **related to visitors** and others who might come in unaware of the intended exposure to the searching of the Holy Spirit, so that a general command for unclean spirits to depart from people filling an auditorium would then be applied to people who *want* deliverance AND people who *don't*. **Some may not be Christians** and we know from God's Word that the unclean spirit that departs may well take back in seven other spirits worse than himself when and where the opportunity presents itself, that is, where the HOLY Spirit has not replaced it.

Consequently a general command for unclean spirits to come out of the congregation **may present some difficulties at open-to-the-public meetings** where people may be unsaved, or unaware as to the nature of the meeting and the direction it may take. However, these difficulties are not insurmountable - indeed they may lead to further blessing.

Two possible solutions for normal (worship) meetings open to the public are offered for your consideration:

(iii) SPECIFIC COMMANDS.

The commands issued at the beginning with the opening prayers may be made in specific terms e.g. "Every remaining unclean spirit *named and commanded out by me in the past* is to manifest now - quickly and quietly and depart continuously throughout the course of this meeting!" All such commands would be given in Jesus' Name, of course.

This order is therefore directed **only at the unclean spirits in those people who have been previously counselled,** (i.e. have requested the ministry at a private counselling session and therefore have already received some ministry) and therefore new visitors should not be adversely affected. Thus deliverance commands would be directed only at those who specifically sought this ministry previously. Any other deliverance that is received because of the Power of God on the meeting would be purely by the grace of God just as indeed happens now in most Christian spiritual meetings, but only very few are aware of it.

(iv) EVANGELISM

If we view a meeting not simply as an ALL-Christian group but a mixture of both Christians and non-Christian (that is, people not yet committed to Jesus Christ as their Saviour and Lord), we could see it as an opportunity for both deliverance AND evangelism.

This would perhaps lead the minister-in-charge to give an opportunity (or several opportunities) to those present to say the "sinner's prayer" of repentance and faith, either by giving them the lead from the front or by inviting them to come forward for counselling. If this is done and the Spirit begins to move in saving, delivering and healing power, then so be it. **We ought not to hold up the blessing of the many because of**

the continued rebellion of the few, and as we have said before, it is God who is working His mighty works; who will try to shorten His arm? Under the sovereignty of God, perhaps some will receive deliverance first, and with various spiritual blocks removed, then be enabled to receive Jesus as their Lord.

In any event, deliverance was a public "sidewalk" matter during Jesus' earthly ministry, and probably will be again in the last of the last days, but for now, we return to discussing ministry in private groups.

(b) PRIVATE GROUP

To begin the ministry, one experienced deliverance counsellor can perhaps oversee four or five subjects satisfactorily (although I have come to believe that deliverance should always be ministered by counsellors in pairs, at least whenever possible), but two experienced counsellors could possibly minister to a group of twelve **to begin.** On this rather arbitrary and cautious numerical basis, I feel that one or two sessions of perhaps one-and-a-half hours ministry each per week, could be made available to your church members and would be within the spiritual capabilities of most persons who felt led to serve the Lord in the deliverance ministry. Again, I repeat that these suggestions are for **beginning** a group.

Obviously some ministers will feel "drained" more quickly than others - some will be "stirred up" because they need deliverance themselves - and some will not seek replenishment from the Lord in the way they should. **The ministers will need lots of praise, plenty of fellowship, lots of prayer and plenty of the Word** fed into their souls to maintain their spiritual strength over the long term.

Likewise the subjects may find that two sessions per week are ample. Changes will be taking place in their personality. They will experience confusion and uncertainty because all that is black and ugly within them will be thoroughly stirred up. Thus they may manifest a side to their personality they never knew existed before. However, they will normally be able to recognise this because you will have forewarned them, but in a positive way, underlining the victories. **They need to understand what is happening,** and thus be keener than ever to be free of the blackness permanently.

Family ministry

For this reason **we used to prefer** that only one adult in a family receive ministry at a time, so that the subject could have the support and encouragement of the other adult members in the household while they are being cleansed. Most families can support one "patient" at a time, but should husband and wife receive ministry in the same season, things can get a little touchy.

My own general preference for family ministry has been "one adult at time" to commence, and see how they cope. But lately this has been overthrown by the Holy Spirit's correction; I believe **because the Time is too short.** We cannot afford to hold back ANYONE'S cleansing at this time in history, in spite of any difficulties. Provided we minister the ministry of Christ according to scriptural *principles,* the methodology is left to the minister to discern the leading of the Holy Spirit according to the needs of the situation. In fact, this whole section is plainly on procedure about which the scriptures are silent and we are continuously thrown back on the wisdom and leading of the Holy Spirit in every situation. So perceive the dangers and ask for wisdom - believe you have it, and decide accordingly. I don't care if you ignore this whole section on procedure, if you have something better from the Spirit.

In the early stages of group ministry it is better *not* to have anyone present without your invitation or approval. **It is a private meeting.** Later, as your anointing of gifts and power from the Lord increases, you may include public meetings in your programme, to which any seeker may come. This certainly means that satanic agencies which have special destructive commissions against your ministry will enter the meetings. **This will spark things up in a way you did not intend** - but, provided the ministers have a mature level of the use of the gifts of the Spirit and know their "authority over ALL the power of the enemy," there is no reason to be alarmed.

Warning

From this you will understand *it is very desirable that experience be obtained in private meetings before public meetings are even considered.* Remember there can be no preparation of the subjects if strangers are allowed into public meetings and a highly developed gift of discernment will be desirable, if not essential.

So, until this experience and development is realised, the meetings at which deliverance commands are given may need to be private rather than public. Non-members of the fellowship (e.g. referrals from other assemblies) may need to be counselled beforehand, being carefully prepared for the type of ministries likely to affect them, and if they wish to attend, perhaps some form of (non-transferable) door-pass could be given to them at their interview, or they could arrive in the company of a member of your fellowship.

There may be some un-informed criticism about the "exclusive" nature of the meeting from people who do not understand, but what is new about that? The army that chooses its own terms, conditions and battle-ground will experience the sweeter victories!

(c) **PUBLIC GROUP WITH A CONTINUOUS DELIVERANCE AND RESTORATION (D. AND R.) PROGRAM.**

Search and Destroy

Christian leaders in the past have tended to "turn a blind eye" to the demonic problems of their people. The general policy seems to have been "If a demon confronts me I deal with it (in Jesus' Name), but I don't go looking for them". It sounds wise and safe and very time-saving for busy leaders, but is that really the way to prosecute the war? Has there been any war in the history of mankind that has been won by ignoring the enemy or by purely defensive measures? – Or by these measures practised by Christians today? Perhaps we should re-write the Scriptures to read "... **I will build my Church and Hades shall not prevail against it's gates**" - which puts the church in the defensive role and Hades in the aggressor's role. (Most Christians will know that Matthew 16:18 really presents the Church as attacking the gates of Hades, not Hades attacking the gates of the Church).

So, for many leaders the "policy" is to let people stay bound in spiritual chains and suffer year after year, unable to fulfil their potential in Christ for true discipleship. The "policy" is to be careful not to look too hard for spiritual enemies - the real problems their people carry - because if they do, they might find them!

Is this the way to prepare the people of God, the Church of God, for the coming of their Lord?

A regular program prosecutes the war of the Lord, for the Lord. Is He not Lord of Hosts (Armies) and are we not His soldiers? Should we not call on the Holy Spirit to search out and destroy the enemy within us and our people? (Ps. 139:23-24). At the very least a regular program gives an implicit invitation and opportunity to troubled Christians who are crying out for help, and may cause others who are not so desperate to reflect on their own spiritual state as well.

A regular program of D. and R. is necessary in order to wage continuous, "ruthless", effective warfare for the cleansing of the children of God **today.**

Private Group to Public Group

I think I have already hinted at the probability that, with the growing experience of the ministers, together with increasing awareness amongst Christians of the spiritual chains which still bind them, the small private group will eventually emerge as a public full-scale D. and R. program.

It will still be "Christians only" or for those who are desirous of becoming a Christian because everyone in group deliverance should be required early in the meeting to pray a prayer of commitment to the Lord Jesus. So, if someone is not a committed Christian before the meeting they should certainly be one soon after the meeting begins. (See sample in the section, OPENING PRAYERS).

The difference is, of course, that **with the increase of experience comes discernment, authority and greater anointing** from the Lord on the minister, which makes a large group no more "difficult" than a small private group, although it is always wise to have trusted and mature colleagues available to assist you, if and when necessary.

My wife Verlie and I now find that there is no limit (remember T.L Osborn?) to the number of people we can minister to with our weekly program – praise the Lord!

So then, let us now consider the obvious benefits of a regular weekly D. and R. program.

THE VALUE OF A CONTINUOUS DELIVERANCE
and
RESTORATION MINISTRY PROGRAM

FOR SUFFERERS:

1   Meets a Christian's need for real and effective cleansing, giving Christians the opportunity to OBEY the command to be

CLEANSED and PURIFIED. (James 4 : 7-8 , 2 Cor 7:1).

2. Gives the Holy Spirit the opportunity to dig deeper and deeper (Ps. 139:23 – 24, Jer. 17:9 – 10). We're talking MAJOR changes!!

IT'S STARTING TO GET DEEP

3. Develops true faith (trust) and commitment to the Lord.

    If we are not prepared to let the Holy Spirit over and through our soulish area (mind and emotions) in order to expose and dig out every unclean thing, then our level of discipleship must be questioned (Luke 9:62).

4. We share in the Word of God and worship with other Christians walking the same narrow Way. Entering such spiritual warfare together develops unity in spirit and purpose. Together we develop enormous group strength in Christ Jesus (Eph. 4:3-6, Heb. 12:1-2,1 Pet. 2:5).

5. A regular program means:

    a) Consistent *commitment* to time and place - ENDURANCE

    b) Regular *teaching* from the Word of God which builds up the Kingdom of God after deliverance has torn down the kingdoms of darkness (Matt. 7:24-27,12:25-28).

     c)   Real spiritual strengthening and growth, which accelerates SANCTIFICATION into Christlikeness (2 Tim. 3:16-17, Heb. 5:12-14).

6.   Overcomes ALL deception. **Every unclean thing is exposed and expelled sooner or later** (John 2:23-3:3, 1Tim. 4:1) if the program is followed faithfully.

7.   Essential for this End-Time of history to ENSURE MEMBERSHIP in the Five Wise Maidens (Matt. 25:1-13).

FOR MINISTERS:

1.   Enormously time-saving. For example, if you ministered to 30 people a week, then:

    30 x 1 hour individual sessions are replaced by:

    $1 \times 2\frac{1}{2}$ hour session (a saving of $27\frac{1}{2}$ hours a week).

    Redeems the time for the Christian minister (Eph. 5:15-16).

2.   Also avoids lengthy interviews and discussions and never-ending counselling sessions. Gets down to 'DOING' rather than 'TALKING'. (1Cor. 4:20, James 1:22-25). One girl in Malaysia wrote to me and said **"I need ministry. I have been counselled to death!"**

3.   More enjoyable format, with plenty of PRAISE and opportunity for the WORD, prophecy etc. Refreshing - not normally exhausting or much more draining than a one-on-one session (Neh. 8:10, Isaiah 40:31). Certainly much less draining than 30 single sessions!

4.   Greatly increases the **anointing** on/of the ministers - **authority, power, discernment** etc.

5.	Invites and gives freedom to the Holy Spirit to deal with each person individually and personally - and powerfully. He blows where He wills (John 3:8).

	God is therefore not limited to the limitations of the flesh of His servants (I Sam. 14:6, Revelation of T.L. Osborn).

6.	"Confines" the ministry to a set time and place, to which needy enquirers can be invited. Choosing the battleground! This avoids many untimely interruptions to a minister's work-day (emergencies excepted), and allows for serious preparation by prayer and fasting, and refreshment after.

7.	Makes ministry available to ALL Christians without discrimination or embarrassment.

God is no respecter of persons

* Jew or Greek (Gentile) - Acts 10:34-35, Rom. 2:10-11.
* Rich or poor		- James 2
* Servant or master	- Eph. 6:5-9,cf. Gal. 3:27-28.

Summary

In summary what we are saying is that most deliverance ministries will progress through a number of stages, probably beginning with an **individual (singular) deliverance session for one person** which is continued over several weeks. This person will probably bring in others with needs, as they bear witness, so that one way or another the weekly single deliverance session will become a **small private group.**

Eventually, by God's grace and power, the gifts and the enquiries will increase to the point where you won't be able to check out every needful enquirer or sufferer BEFORE the meetings, and the "patients" you already have will have to do that for you before they invite the new ones along. They will use the wisdom which comes from above, if you ask them to, and you teach them how they can encourage and help others in bondage.

When things get to this stage, a minister ought to seriously consider a total assembly situation, with **continuous deliverance during full worship meetings,** or, even better, a **separate continuous Deliverance and Restoration meeting and program** open to all Christians.

Have a look at this general format for a Deliverance and Restoration meeting.

(d) SAMPLE D. & R. MEETING

(Two and a half hours - plus supper fellowship)

1. Opening worship song.
2. Introductory remarks (see Final Instructions – page 28).
3. Worship song.
4. Opening Prayers and binding instructions to unclean spirits by the Pastor or the Deliverance Minister.
5. Ministry by the Deliverance Minister, exercising discernment and authority, from anywhere in the hall. (Approximately 30-40 minutes).
6. Worship songs (2).
7. Message (Pastor) while the D.M. continues ministry with the laying-on-of-hands, as led. (30-40 minutes)
8. Intermission (stretch legs etc.) - (3-5 minutes).
9. Worship songs and/or Holy Communion. Ministry continues throughout. (30 minutes).
10. Binding and closing prayers (including praying for the FILLING of the Holy Spirit for EVERYONE).
11. Worship song with thank-offering.
12. Thank-offering prayer.
13. Closing worship song.
14. Blessing.
15. Supper, interviews and packing up (60 minutes).

(iii) GATHERED TOGETHER.

You have announced the place and the time. You have prepared yourself and the sufferers (refer to Book 1) and now they are sitting before you in the church or church hall, or wherever, chatting happily (the new ones a little nervously?) in expectation. They see you and they trust you. They know you love Jesus and you love them, and they are about to experience the delivering and miraculous power of the risen Christ cleansing out His (their) temples. They have had trouble getting there - satan has done all in his power - all he has been permitted to do, to stall, hinder and stop those Christians arriving; but they are there in front of you - eager, expectant and grateful. So they are sitting before you, prepared and ready as they will ever be. Your counsellors are ready to minister to individuals as you direct, having first made ready **all the necessary practical matters,** such as:

i)   All sound-proofing is in place - over windows and doors as necessary.

ii)   Clean small plastic buckets easily available for those who will need them to cough or retch into.

iii)   If they need a bucket, they will certainly need paper tissues or cloths for wiping of noses and mouths.

iv)   Electronic and musical equipment ready (optional):

a) microphones for the ministers, mainly for speaking clearly to the unclean, but also for directing counsellors. We don't use this now, as Verlie's anointing and clear voice make it un-necessary, so they are used by the preacher and the lead singers.

b) tape recorder ready for playing deliverance commands or praise and worship. This provides enormous vocal support and "saves" your voice, which can be reserved for commands at critical moments, and for less common spirits. **Live music and worship is even better than tapes.**

c) We also like to tape record the meetings for checking of details afterwards, and for security reasons. If there is any drama at the meeting you will have a record of who said what to whom, and why. This gives no place to the devil to work his slander (Eph. 4:27).

v) Any other practical matters, depending on your set-up.

Opening the Meeting

It is a good idea to open the meeting with a worship song or two and save your introductory guidance and remarks until the meeting is well under way.

The reason for this is that your opening comments will be very, very important to those who have come to a Deliverance and Restoration meeting for the first time - and usually these NEW PEOPLE will be the ones who come in LATE!

Whatever the reason - nervousness? Finding the meeting place? Parking? You can be sure that many NEWCOMERS will be LATECOMERS.

How many times have I given my introduction to people who don't really need it (because they have heard it before) only to have a newcomer enter soon after I have finished.

They come in and sit down nervously and look around, wondering what to do, while I roll my eyes up to Heaven and mutter, "They've done it to me again, Lord!"

If a newcomer comes in so late as to miss praying the curse-breaking prayer I lead them outside the meeting again and explain the need to pray the prayer with me right then and there. Only then do I take them back into the meeting again for ministry.

FINAL INSTRUCTIONS

Practical Steps

The subjects can assist immensely by *relaxing physically,* and loosening tight clothing, removing ties, bracelets, watch bands and shoes - anything that might interfere with their blood circulation, because the battle is in the soul and the soul is in the blood (Lev. 17:11,14). They should sit straight but loosely in their chairs and avoid crossing their legs, or clenching or clasping hands. The best position is to have the hands palm upwards and open, resting on their thighs. They should "hang loose", with their spirits and minds centred on Jesus. Deliverance can take place at any moment now, and indeed for some of them deliverance will have already commenced earlier in the day with spirits fleeing at the very prospect of ministry to come. For "old hands" ministry may begin the moment the journey to the deliverance meeting commences, or it may be when they first step into the deliverance room, or your familiar voice is heard. **Usually spirits that leave prior to actual ministry are quite weak,** and no embarrassment or drama is experienced.

Welcome

Immediately after I have welcomed people to the meeting I declare that.

"This is a Deliverance and Restoration meeting, called in the Name of our Lord Jesus Christ."

I then explain that **deliverance ministry tears down** the pollution within us and should always be followed by **restoration, the building up** of the Kingdom (Rule) of God in every part of our being.

Running away

It is as well to warn sufferers, especially those new to your meetings, that the enemy may attempt to take them out of the meeting. A person may feel a rising anger or fear, or even panic, and find their legs wanting to rush them outside and away. They may develop a thumping headache and little voices may begin to whisper "What are you doing here? You feel terrible. This place is evil. Get out quick!"

These enemy attacks can take place at any time during a meeting, so if you warn the people early in the meeting, they will be better equipped to resist. I tell them plainly that when an urge comes upon them to run away they are to **hold onto their seats tightly** and don't give in to their legs which want to get up and run.

If they run away **they lose the battle** on the day and will have to wait for another opportunity to get rid of that spirit.

If they can hold onto their seats - no matter how they feel - the unclean spirit will go out of the meeting without them, and they win.

The manifesting unclean spirit will go out of the meeting one way or the other. The only question is whether it will take the sufferer with it - or not!

Your final instructions to people will include a warning NOT to worry about their manners. **People who fight against and hold back coughs, sneezes, yawns, retching etc. are fighting against the ministry of the Spirit.** That is so important, it is worth repeating. People who fight and hold back coughs, sneezes, yawns, retching etc. are fighting against the ministry of the Spirit. They are to forget their manners in these circumstances and instead, should help the spiritual poison out of their systems. If their nose dribbles, they should let it dribble - Praise the Lord! If their eyes water, let them - Praise the Lord! They should keep their hands away as much as possible! *They and their spirits are to be focussed UNDIVIDEDLY ON JESUS.* If their chin or ear tickles - let it. Such things can be attended to by the counsellors where absolutely necessary, or alternatively, they should wait unit the end of the deliverance session, when they can mop up and/or scratch themselves to their hearts content. People who can obey these directions make the quickest progress because

(i)   They do not interfere with what God is doing.
(ii)   They overrule their pride (because they may feel they look a mess and others can see), and
(iii)   Their spirit is not distracted from the Lord!

These instructions having been given, it is time to pray.

5. 2 OPENING PRAYERS

What are we going to pray? Well, **whosoever shall call upon the Name of the Lord "shall be saved"** (Acts 2:21) Or, if you prefer the prophet Joel's rendition, **"shall be delivered."** So it really amounts basically to calling upon the name of the Lord, and that Name is Jesus! We need His Presence!

(i) THE MINISTER'S PRAYER

The Minister does this in four ways.

(a) **We pray for faith to move mountains.** Now, you may not be facing very strong spirits. They might only be "mole hills" in comparison, but you may not know that. One afternoon during ministry we were attacking many mole hills and then we came to a mountain, a strong spirit of fear. It gave us considerable trouble but, praise be to God, eventually we were given victory. This is normal and so you will need faith to move mountains.

You know the scriptures as well as I do. Paul said - **"If I have all faith, so as to remove mountains ..."** (1 Cor. 13:2). He describes it as being all faith. "All things are possible to him who believes" and we are not to doubt but to believe for the thing we ask for to be given to us.

(b) **The second thing we need to pray for is the power of God the Holy Spirit.** We need to be filled continuously with the Spirit because we cannot afford to minister in the weakness of the flesh. If you minister in the weakness of the flesh, it is possible to get a transfer of spirits and nobody can afford that. You must minister in the power of the Holy Spirit of God, so pray that He will clothe you with power from on High.

(c) **The minister also ought to pray for protection** from the evil one and all his spirits; we need to claim **the covering of the blood of the Passover Lamb,** for Paul says that **Christ is our Passover Lamb sacrificed for us** (1 Cor. 5:7), and also we need to claim the promise of God. **"I will keep you and preserve you from all evil in your going out and in your coming in, from this time forth and forever more"** - and the promise of the Lord Jesus Christ, **"Lo, I am with you always even to the close of the age"** - and another beautiful promise at the end of Jesus' words in Luke 10:19, **"And nothing shall by any means hurt you."** You will remember from Chapter 3, Book 1, that this is a very strong phrase which means that "nothing shall never (lit. not not) hurt you." If the Greeks wanted to use a strong negative, they used a double or even triple negative. If I use a double negative in English, I get a positive (e.g. "I'm not going nowhere" means "I am going somewhere") but it doesn't work that way in New Testament Greek, so the meaning is that **"No thing shall not not or never hurt you,"** if you will excuse the literal "English" rendition. This, of course, is a very emphatic TRIPLE negative and gives great force to Jesus' promise that we shall be mightily protected as we preach the Kingdom of God, and as we see the Kingdom of God coming upon polluted people, displacing the kingdom of satan, as satan's demons are cast out (Matt. 12:26-28).

(d) Fourthly, **we claim or take the authority of a child of God** over all the power of the enemy in Jesus' name. Do you remember the full verse? **"Behold I give you authority to tread on serpents and scorpions and over all the power of the enemy and nothing shall hurt you"** (Luke 10:19). That is powerful and if you *believe* it, that is even more powerful. It is one of the basic verses that we use in the ministry, and we claim it; God honours it and makes it real, and for that we thank Him.

In summary we have said that the deliverance minister should pray for, claim and thank the Lord for these four basic spiritual weapons:

1) **Faith to move mountains** (Mark 9:23, 11:22-24, 1 Cor. 13:2).

2) **The Power of God the Holy Spirit** (Luke 4:14; 5:17; 6:19; 8:46; 24:49; Acts 6:8, 2 Cor. 6:7, Eph. 5:18, 1 Peter 1:5).

3) **The Protection of the Blood of Jesus** (Exod. 12, link with 1 Cor. 5:7, Ps. 121:7-8, Matt. 28:20, Luke 10:19, Heb. 13:5).

4) **The Authority of a child of God** (Luke 10:19, Matt. 18:18; 28:18-19). (See also studies on Authority - Chapter 3, section 1, Book 1; Chapter 5,3; this book; and Chapter 9,3 (iii), Book 3).

(ii) PUBLIC GROUP PRAYER

The persons who are receiving ministry need to pray along the following lines.

(a) **Pray for forgiveness for themselves,** because we do not want any barrier of sin coming between them and the Lord in any way. It is a good thing to wash away every stain and spot of sin with prayer before we receive ministry. James 5:16 says to Christians, **"Confess your sins to one another that you may be healed."** That spells it out clearly enough for anybody and it "clears the air" to have the forgiveness of your sins right up-to-date, bringing things right up to the minute with the Lord so that you can indeed be accounted righteous, for **"the prayer of a righteous person has great power in its effect"** (James 5:16).

Why do we suggest praying for forgiveness today when you did this yesterday? Simply because the Lord's prayer is designed as a daily prayer ("Give us this day ...") and it includes a prayer for our forgiveness ("... And forgive us our trespasses ..."). If one part of the Lord's prayer is to be prayed daily, surely that would apply to the whole prayer. Some theologians think because Christians are "in Christ" we are continuously forgiven without having to ask, but I think they have outsmarted themselves, and have been persuaded to presume on their sonship, like sons do with their earthly fathers.

How rich a blessing there is for those who keep their communication lines open and "running hot". Let us pray like the Lord says, and we cannot go wrong.

Also **it is necessary to forgive others.** Maybe you think *you* have forgiveness, but you haven't forgiven somebody else. You CANNOT hold hatreds if you are asking the Lord to remove your sins; you cannot really hold resentments against anybody else and expect to be healed (James 5:16, Matt. 6:12-15).

(b) The subject ought to **declare the renunciation of the devil** entirely; **"He who confesses and forsakes his transgression will obtain mercy"** says Proverbs 28:13, and Isaiah 55:7 says, **"Let the wicked forsake his ways".**

It is desirable for the subject to renounce the devil, the powers of darkness and all their works, and then,

(c) **Ask the Lord to break every curse,** chain or shackle

about them, and

(d) **Make a declaration of allegiance.** An easy way to remember it is:

F	orsaking
A	ll
I	
T	ake or Trust
H	im

Putting all this together with the subject's initial confession of sin, we have the deliverance minister leading those gathered before him for deliverance, **repeating after him** a prayer something like this:

> Dear Lord Jesus,
>
> I am a sinner and I acknowledge my sin before you. I repent and I ask you to forgive me and cleanse me from every stain and spot of sin.
>
> Thank you for dying on the Cross to save me and cleanse me.
>
> I renounce the devil, the power of darkness and all their works and acknowledge you, Lord Jesus, as my Lord and my God.
>
> I ask you to break every chain and shackle about me, remove every foul curse from me, even to the third and fourth generation; heal me and deliver me.
>
> I forgive those who have hurt me and wrongfully used me and I ask *You* to forgive them also. Please take every root of bitterness out of my heart forever.
>
> Search me, O Lord, in my innermost parts and cleanse me

from every kingdom of sin, and set me free to worship you and serve as you lead me.

Fully fill me and restore me by your Holy Spirit that I may be the person you want me to be.

Thank you, Lord Jesus[1]

The above is a fairly complete example of a Full Salvation prayer and obviously there may be times when the Holy Spirit deletes or adds prayer points according to the leading He gives you.

5.3 INSTRUCTIONS TO DEMONS (UNCLEAN SPIRITS).

The group seeking deliverance is sitting in front of you, and both you and they have talked to the Lord, and you all know He is in your midst. As they raise their faces and eyes (from prayer), some will already begin to manifest uncleanness, and here and there, a pair of eyes will begin to glare at you, hostility, tears, fear, etc. I remember a Spanish lady who couldn't understand a word of English, yet every time the prayers concluded and the time came to bind and instruct all the demons, the demon in her would begin to wail and scream until she was put under the power of God (we'll explain more about that later). She couldn't understand anything with her mind but the things *in* her understood only too well what was about to happen.

(i) BINDING THE POWERS OF DARKNESS.

(a) You know that you have power to bind and power to loose in the Name of Jesus and that you cannot rob the strong man's house unless you first bind the strong man - then you can rob his house (Matt. 12:29; 18:18). So, before any other commands are given, the "strong men" in the group are BOUND TO BE TOTALLY INACTIVE so that we can plunder their houses of all

---

1   See Appendix E-Book 1 for another curse-breaking prayer.

their kingdoms of spirits - *IN JESUS' MIGHTY NAME!*

That is the *FIRST* command and, according to Jesus, may make the difference between failure and success.

(b) Then we give a blanket command to all the various kingdoms of spirits within the sufferers and we verbally *BIND THEM TO OBEY EVERY DIRECTION AND COMMAND OF THE MINISTER(S).* They are very firmly charged and adjured in Jesus' Name to do so.[1]

This having been done, we are now able to tell them what we want them to do and where to go etc.

(ii) THE COMMAND *"COME OUT ...!"*

(a) All unclean spirits are commanded to manifest (show themselves) quickly and to leave the subjects. *This is the very heart of the ministry - "You unclean spirit(s) of...... "COME OUT IN JESUS NAME!"* or "LOOSE HIM/HER IN JESUS' NAME!"

These days we prefer to use "Loose" rather than "COME OUT" as this re-affirms the authority of the Christian to bind and to loose.

This whole book is written around those last five word commands. You may use other words but they should have the same meaning as those commands - an executive command issued in the Name above all names, to whom has been given all authority in Heaven and on earth.

In a **group situation,** one person can issue this command to many by raising the voice level, but in a **one-to-one situation** wear and tear on the voice box can be saved considerably by placing your mouth close to an ear and whispering the command. Whispering or talking quietly into the ear drum carries all the force and volume you need, PROVIDED you

---

1   Audio cassette tapes available on this.

speak crisply, meaningfully, and maintain your authority. In group situations and where a team of Christians is present to support the deliverance minister, the supporting counsellors should be instructed to minister quietly into the ear drum whenever possible. This will not only save their physical voices, but also keep the noise level of the meeting down to a minimum, and contribute to better control and therefore more effective deliverance for everyone. **A word of warning** - make sure that counsellors **do not speak LOUDLY into an ear drum.** When that happens, even a normal speaking level of volume can sound like a clap of thunder to the hearer.

(b) The demons are ordered to LEAVE QUICKLY, QUIETLY AND CONTINUOUSLY, without causing any fuss or distress and go to their appointed place (nominated by you if not previously done so - say 100 miles - and never to return - Mark 9:25). They are to be silent inactive and harmless (Luke 10:19) until they reach their appointed place, and they are never to enter a blood-bought Christian ever again. In this way the church (the Bride of Christ) will get cleaner and cleaner for the Rapture, and the world can get as filthy as it desires for Judgement Day (cf. Rev. 22:10-12). We will discuss **where to send demons** in detail in the next section.

Music

You will remember that in Book 1, Chapter 2, we suggested that the context of singing praises and preaching the Word of God was highly supportive to the deliverance ministry. One reason is because it is so important for sufferers to keep their spirits fixed on the Lord as much as possible while they receive ministry, and we can best achieve this objective over long periods of time by having the group singing the Word of God put to music during the ministry.

By singing scripture choruses they are feeding their souls with the Word of God, keeping their spirits on Jesus, and praising the Lord, all at the same time. The ministers, too, can join in as the Holy Spirit leads. It is a most enjoyable way of ministering and obtaining deliverance. Because musicians themselves quickly become affected by the Power of God and are often rendered incapable of playing cohesive music (because they are present in the meeting to receive deliverance also), I have sometimes found the only way to provide music throughout the 1 1/2 - 2 1/2 hours[1] of ministry, is to *play cassette tapes of selected anointed worship,* with the words of the scripture choruses projected onto a blank wall or screen by an overhead projector. Such anointed background worship may be commenced at the very beginning of the meeting, turning down the speakers during the prayers and binding commands, and resuming the singing as soon as practical. However, **if your musicians can play "live" music for you, that is much better** for control of the meeting. **Pastors should allow the deliverance minister to control the music as a weapon of war** (2 Chron. 20:21-22).

Scripture readings

When ministering to only one or two sufferers where perhaps constant singing is inappropriate, and yet where a long period of ministry is probable, it is a good idea to command the spirits to continue to depart during the reading of the Word of God (may I remind you there are 150 Psalms praising God). This makes the ministry much more interesting and less tedious to the minister, who may otherwise be faced with the prospect of repeating "Come out in Jesus' Name" with a few variations for some considerable time. The ministry might be new and exciting to you (and it still is to me), but if you use the same words of loosing hour after hour, and week after week, you may find it difficult to maintain concentration over the long term. You need to look at some way whereby you can minister effectively, and at the same time not only minister Jesus to the subject but minister to yourself. Reading the scriptures out loud is

---

1   Meetings where deliverance commands are issued audibly throughout, without the context of praise, are perhaps best kept to 1 1/2 hours. However, deliverance ministered DURING WORSHIP can go on for much longer periods.

extremely helpful to me; I find that I receive something from the ministry as well as the person being prayed for. As for singing of choruses by groups, I receive a great blessing out of that too.

(iii) NAMES, CHARACTERS AND USE OF DISCERNMENT.

We usually need to **name the name** or **identify the character** of the demons that have been revealed by discernment or at counselling time; or alternatively in unusual situations, we have to get them to name themselves. **Don't mix names over-much with one-to-one ministry.** It is certainly not wise to have one person ministering against one name in one ear, and someone else confuse them with another name in the other ear. That is not very helpful; it is best to unite your attack and generally keep to the one spirit at a time - and don't change your attack unless you have unity with your co-workers. **You need to be purposeful and united at all times.** It is here that you put into effect all that you have learnt about DISCERNING OF SPIRITS.

"Lessons from Perseverance"

When considering the length of time the ministry sometimes takes, the efficient use of discernment (or lack of it) has to be taken into account; but bear in mind that VERY OFTEN THE LORD TAKES US THE LONG WAY AROUND to obtain the victory. For example, it took the Hebrews **40 years to move out of Egypt and into the Promised Land of Canaan,** when geographically it should only have taken a matter weeks. "But," you say, "that was a unique or special situation. They needed to learn so much about faith and trusting God, about the Law of God and obedience to it." Yes, that is true for them and it is also true for us. Special situations or not, the point I am making is that, with spiritual things, quick "solutions" promise much but may give NOTHING. However, when the Lord takes us the LONG way around; THOSE WHO ARE FAITHFUL GET THERE AND RECEIVE EVERYTHING PROMISED! **We, too,** have to learn about faith and trusting God. **We, too,** have to receive and be obedient to the Law of Christ as revealed in the *New* Testament and live by it, or **we, too,** may die in a spiritual wilderness and never enter the blessing that God has prepared for us.

We also have to bear in mind, when it comes to naming spirits in order of priority for removal, that no two battles and no two kingdoms of unclean spirits appear to be always the same. Illustrating from the Hebrews' invasion of the kingdoms of Canaan, the walls of Jericho fell flat when the Hebrews followed God's battle-plan to the letter, but after that, other kingdoms were overthrown by ambush and various other tactics. No two conquests appear to have been the same. Sometimes the Lord's battle tactics can seem to cause delays. To illustrate again: it took seven (7) days for Jericho's walls to fall flat and the Hebrews to take the city (Joshua 6:12 f.). Someone might say that if the Hebrews had stormed the city on the first day, it would have fallen within 24 hours - three days at the latest - and they could have saved themselves four days or more on their invasion timetable. We who are Christians would say that God knows best and His way is the best way. Not only does it appear that the Hebrews did not suffer casualties but God's "slower" way obtained the victory whereas man's "quicker" way would have resulted, at best, in heavy casualties; or, at worst, a siege lasting months, and probably ending even in defeat. In other words, what seems to be a quicker way leads to nowhere but **God's way (fast or slow) is really quickest and surest!**

Applying this principle to the deliverance ministry means that when God gives discernment on a certain problem, THAT is the way to minister. You may know what the *obvious* problems is, for example - **epilepsy,** but the Lord may give you discernment of **spiritism.** If you minister His way you'll get rid of the spiritism, the epilepsy, and whatever else lies in between. If you just tackle what is obvious—your way—you may find yourself on a spiritual treadmill that leads nowhere (Prov. 3:5).

Talking about discernment, have you ever closely considered

the case of **the man with the Legion?** Just take a few moments to look at the biblical evidence:

1)   He didn't live in houses like other   Luke 8:27-29
      people, but in the tombs   Mark 5:3

2)   He ran around naked   Luke 8:27

3)   The spirits in him were quite   Mark 5:12
      happy to transfer into swine

4)   He was very fierce and very, very   Matt 8:28
      strong   Mark 5:3

5)   He often cried out with a loud voice   Mark 5:5-7

6)   He cut himself with stones   Mark 5:5-7

7)   After his deliverance he is   Mark 5:15
      described as being "in his right mind"

All the above information is, of course, very revealing about the nature of the unclean spiritual kingdoms that made up the empire called "Legion," but how did they get in? How did he become such a severe case? Most important of all, **which is the root, the cause upon which all the rest of his uncleanness was built upon?**

The answer is idolatory. You will probably respond to that suggestion in one of two ways. You may say, "How come?" - or, "Of course the root cause is idolatory - isn't it always? Every problem we have can be traced back to forsaking our Creator and seeking after other gods. For example, Adam and Eve disbelieved God and believed the serpent in the first occult exercise in human history, because they sought to become gods themselves (Gen. 3:5)".

That is true; all human problems can be traced back to the root sin of idolatory - serving other gods rather than Almighty God, but what kind of idolatory was at the root of the problems in the man with the Legion.? The Bible gives us the answer. **His problems were hereditary** and he was a descendant of BAAL worshippers. Why do we say that? The clue is in Mark 5:5 where he is described as constantly bruising or cutting[1] himself with stones. Why did he do that? The poor man himself would not have understood why he did such a stupid, self-destructive act, but the unclean spirits in him had been transferred down the blood-line through many generations from the prophets of BAAL, who used to mutilate themselves in this way in order to appease the wrath of, obtain the approval of, and get some "action" from their miserable god (1 Kings 18:28). He was simply under their control. His actions were not sane or reasonable but flowed from the idolatrous rituals sourced in an earlier century, and were spiritually inspired.

We should not think that the spirit of BAAL is an area of idolatry that does not concern us in Western and/or Christian nations. I remember receiving a 'phone call from a young soldier's wife during my curacy at Kingswood, NSW. She had entered the bathroom while her husband was shaving one morning and was horrified to discover him standing transfixed in front of his shaving mirror, staring at the blood seeping from wounds around his shoulders that he had inflicted upon himself with his razor. This condition is apparently well known in psychiatric circles.

If you doubt that idolatory is the root cause of ALL our ills, perhaps you would **refer to Romans 1:24-32** where it seems to me the apostle **Paul also gives his discernment** on the kingdoms of sin which make up the **homosexual (sodomy)[2]** empire. He says that people suffering from **the homosexual condition (vs. 26-27)** are consequently FILLED with a number

---

1   This Greek New Testament Dictionary explains the meaning as "to cut up, cut in pieces."

2   The homosexual community in Sodom tried to have intercourse with angels who appeared as men (Gen. 19:1-13), and could have been aware that (fallen) angels had committed incubi sexual acts with women (Gen. 6:1-5).

of key **unclean kingdoms (v.29)** which then RESULTS in a range of character defects (vs. 29-31) or what the apostle Paul would call works of the flesh (Gal. 5:19-21). I suggest that you look at the text (Romans 1:18-31) for the spiritual kingdoms, and their physical manifestations, as listed in the chart of Human Pollution.

HUMAN POLLUTION
(Romans 1:18-32)

Verses18-23, 25,28,32)	IDOLATRY	(THE ROOT PROBLEM)

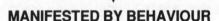

Verses 24,26 27,28B)	SEXUAL LICENCE	(GOD GAVE THEM UP TO THIS)

Verse 29)	FILLED WITH -	(GENERAL DESCRIPTION)

UNRIGHTEOUSNESS - EVIL - COVETOUSNESS - BAD

Verse 29)	FULL OF (KINGDOMS OF)	(SPECIFIC KING-DOMS NAMED)

ENVY - MURDER - GUILE - STRIFE - MALIGNITY

MANIFESTED BY BEHAVIOUR

Verse 29	WHISPERERS	(GOSSIPS,SLANDERERS)
Verse 30	RAILERS	(EVILSPEAKING,NEGATIVE,CRITICAL
	GOD - HATERS	
	INSOLENT	(VIOLENT, INJURIOUS)
	ARROGANT	(HAUGHTY, DISDAINFUL)
	BOASTERS	
	INVENTORS OF EVIL	
	DISOBEDIENT TO PARENTS	
Verse 31	UNDISCERNING	(FOOLISH)
	FAITHLESS	(UN-RELIABLE,FAILURE TO KEEP AGREEMENTS)
	WITHOUT NATURAL AFFECTION	
	UN-MERCIFUL (RUTHLESS)	

There is no doubt in my mind that this scripture passage is a vital revelation of the deep problems in the human soul.

(iv) TALKING WITH DEMONS

(a) THE MESSIANIC SECRET

Should demons be allowed to speak? Well, some pastors say, "No" - because Jesus told demons to be silent in the Gospels. But I suggest to you that it doesn't really matter now because the reason Jesus would not permit the demons to speak then was because they knew Him, they knew He was the Christ, the Son of God (Mark 1:34, 3:11-12). Jesus muzzled them because He did not want the demons revealing Him as the Messiah too soon. He knew if they openly revealed His Messiahship the people would have seized Him and made Him King. There are several instances where Christ backed away from being made King of Israel to avoid bringing about a military confrontation with the local Roman authorities - that was not His purpose. His Kingdom was, and is, not of this world, and so to avoid confusing the crowds and forcing a clash with the Romans so early in His ministry He commanded the demons to be silent (Mark 1:34).

You will notice that doesn't apply in the Legion case because they are well away from everybody in the unclean areas of the tombs. Only the disciples were there and it didn't matter that they knew He was the Messiah. There were only a few swineherdsmen on the hill, quite some distance away and well out of hearing. So I suggest that preventing demons from speaking is no longer necessary. In fact, it is often very helpful if they do speak because they only give each other away. They give their "friends" away; they have no loyalty to each other whatsoever, and while you have control of the situation, then you are in business for the Lord. However, it is very important that you control the conversation and hold fast your authority in Christ. I remember a case where the demons were panicking and saying within the sufferer, "The pattern's breaking up, the pattern's breaking up". That was helpful to us at that time, early in the ministry. It was helpful to know what they were doing and saying. There was another case of one speaking out quite loudly, "I won't go, I won't go, I won't, I won't;" and another, "I HATE this Church!" Well, that was helpful, believe it or not, simply because we were "on to it". There was another case where the spirit was saying, "I'm the last, I'm the last. Yes, I'm the last," or words to that effect, and we said we didn't believe it, was a liar - and just as this one was leaving it called out and said, "Don't get me mate". He gave away the fact that there were others still to remove. Some of the weaker spirits are really quite brainless, but beware of over-confidence in the flesh and the subtlety of others that are very deceitful.

(b) DOUBLE MEANINGS (LUKE 4:31-37, MARK 1:21-28).

One of the problems we have in the Body of Christ today is that unclean spirits can get up and speak in church through all kinds of people, reputable or otherwise, and very few Christians, if any at all, are able to discern it is indeed an unclean spirit that is speaking, even if they disagree with the sentiments expressed.

Where can you find a church committee or council, even a diaconate or eldership (consisting of many members) which has not been infiltrated by enemy (spiritual) agents? This is not meant to be offensive or invite finger pointing but is simply a statement of the truth, as even Jesus' "college" of twelve disciples illustrates. Jesus said to them **"...you are clean, but not all of you"**. - speaking of Judas Iscariot (John 13:10-11).

So what I am saying is that **unclean spirits get plenty of opportunity to parade themselves, simply because they are undetected.** They are allowed to say far too much , and are the number one reason why the Church has been divided and fairly ineffective for nineteen centuries. Whatever the Church or individual Christians have achieved is surely and purely by the overriding and sovereign grace of Almighty God, through Jesus Christ our Lord. Amazing grace indeed.

Is there any scriptural evidence for what I am saying? Yes, there certainly is. I have touched on it before (Book 1) but it is worth repeating. Imagine if you will, your own local assembly. The place is packed and you have a visiting speaker from some foreign country. He is a Christian leader whom, it is said, can perform miracles and he brings to your meeting some unheard-of and mindblowing concepts about the Kingdom of God which don't seem to have much (if any) support **from the scriptures known to you.** The well-trained members of your assembly who have been to Bible or Theological College become uneasy and restless and finally one of them gets to his feet and challenges the visitor, **"What have you to do with us, Jesus of Nazareth** (or Kenneth Copeland of America, or Reinhard Bonnke of South Africa)? Are you trying to destroy the Church with your heresy?" (cf. Mark 1:24).

Perhaps we ought to re-frame our story and put it back into its New Testament setting (Mark 1:21-28, Luke 4:31-37). Let us think of ourselves as a devout Jew in the town of Capernaum when this itinerant Rabbi Jesus comes to visit us, with a reputation of having performed a few miracles preceding Him. But keep in mind He comes from Nazareth (can any good thing come from there?) and His teaching is decidedly controversial. Why, He keeps talking about the Kingdom of God and if the Romans get to hear of it, they "will come and destroy both our holy place and our nation" (John 11:48b). Doesn't He know that the Romans will not tolerate any other King but Caesar? This fellow is dangerous, with a capital "D!"

"Jesus of Nazareth, have you brought your teaching to us so as to destroy us?"

Probably half of the worshippers in the synagogue would have agreed with this caution and cried out, "Amen!"

But then the speaker, still standing on his feet, wants to show that, although he recognises the Rabbi Jesus is speaking dangerously, nevertheless he is a true Jew and will make his commitment to his God and his Messiah, Jesus, regardless of the personal cost and risk to Israel's survival as a semi-autonomous nation - so he declares:

"I know who you are, the Holy One of God!"...

and the other half of the synagogue cries out "Alleluia!"

What does Jesus do? Does He say to the speaker, "Well done, my brother; I can use courageous men like you?" **No.** Does He say, "You are not far from the Kingdom of God?" **No.** Does He say, "Shh! The time is not yet for the uprising of Israel to throw off the yoke of the Roman. Be patient!" **No.** What does Jesus do? To the utter astonishment of everyone present He stops teaching the Word of God and comes down into the assembly and casts out the unclean spirit from the speaker (Mark 1:21-28)! No wonder they were all amazed! They didn't even know the man HAD an unclean spirit, let alone speak under its inspiration - and what he said had made so much sense. Why he (it) even acknowledged that Jesus of Nazareth WAS (and is) the Holy One of God! (cf. Acts 16:17)

Now do you see why I entitled this section **"Double Meanings?"** What the unclean spirit said in the synagogue had a meaning for the Jews living under the heel of the Roman conquerer, but Jesus perceived the REAL meaning, that is, the SPIRITUAL meaning that WE obtain today when reading the scripture because Mark, with hindsight, informs us *early* in the story (v.23) that an unclean spirit is responsible for speaking out. Thus we know from the beginning that the conversation has to do with spiritual, not physical kingdoms.

(c) EXAMPLES OF DOUBLE MEANINGS

Does this kind of double-meaning conversation occur today? it certainly does. **Here are some examples of what unclean spirits say through people,** and which, if you think to be genuine responses, may have the effect of deflecting you from your task:

(i) "I'm getting out of here!"

If you heard these words come from a Christian attending one of your meetings you might be tempted to be discouraged, thinking that your meeting lacked something; but on the contrary, when you perceive this utterance is coming from an unclean spirit, it is very encouraging. It means that the presence of the Lord is so strong that the unclean spirit feels its security and anonymity is threatened, and it will try to take its house well away from the threat as fast as possible. **If you can persuade the Christian to stay,** he or she will probably get a good release as the demon is forced to leave its previous dwelling place (the Christian) in the meeting and depart.

(ii) "What am I doing here?"

If you are holding a deliverance and healing meeting, these words will probably be followed by, "I haven't got unclean spirits (or any demons). I don't need this". This might cause you to pause for a moment but, as these words often pour from a mouth that has earlier told you just the opposite, it is not hard to discern what is happening. These words are usually spoken by someone whom you know to be "loaded".

(iii) "What a lot of tommyrot (or rubbish)!"

(iv) "I don't believe this!"
(No prizes for discerning the spirit of unbelief.)

(v) "This is a madhouse!"

(vi) "You are frightening the life out of me!"

(vii) "I feel terrible!"

You need discernment with this last comment in order to distinguish between the unclean and human spirit. The unclean spirit will be negative and attempting to stop the ministry but the human spirit (with support from the Holy Spirit) will be positive and want you to push on with your ministry. There is a big difference between "I feel terrible, poor me" and "I feed terrible, praise the Name of the Lord," and there are no prizes for knowing which obtains the speedier release.

(viii)   "Nobody loves me" OR "Nobody understands (me)".

It is the old, old story of our tongue, our conversation revealing the spirit which is controlling the mind at a particular time. With a little practice (Heb. 5:13-14) it becomes quite easy, praise the Lord, to discern what kind of spirit with which you are talking.

Where do you send them? It is time to discuss that now.

5. 4 WHERE TO SEND DEMONS

There is very little evidence as to where to send demons and what we have is somewhat sketchy, but the following points are worth nothing :

Preventing their return

We know that Jesus bound one spirit never to return to its previous house again - **"I command you, come out of him and never enter him again".** (Mark 9:25) So we can charge them never to return to the subject or the subject's family again.

They don't like water

Jesus said they wander *the waterless and dry places of the earth* seeking rest. That seems to me to clearly say **they don't like water;** they are free after expulsion to go through the dry places and find themselves another house if they can (Matt. 12:43-45). That is their prerogative in this fallen world. **The Bible teaches only the reincarnation of unclean spirits - but NOT the human spirit!**[1]

1   See "The Re-incarnation Deception" or Book 4 "Discerning Human Nature

Even if there are certain types of spirit which are created to inhabit watery regions and which could be called "demons of the deep", it is probable that such demons only infest marine life, whereas *the unclean spirits referred to by Jesus* were those seeking to inhabit human beings and therefore travelled the land masses of the earth, *avoiding the watery places.*

It is interesting to note that Mrs. Elizabeth Oakland, an English "White" Witch,[1] is quoted as saying she would like to visit her friends in Australia. The difficulty seems to be in getting there. "My broomstick is quite adequate for ... here, but... it is hard for a witch to cross water, you know". (Sunday Telegraph 22/1/84) Yes, we can well realise why, thanks to the Word of God!

Now, assuming that the demons seeking to pollute mankind hate water, we can make a number of confirmatory observations:

(i)   A lady receiving deliverance from **religious spirits** sailed for overseas. She reported upon her return that she continued to experience deliverance daily on the high seas, and especially when she went swimming during stopovers.

(ii)   When I went to apply for a week-end job as a Catechist in my college-student days at a church situated on a North Shore beach many years ago, I was told, "We are a pretty easy lot to get along with - **like most of the seaside suburbs".** The observation was made by the minister who interviewed me that people living on the city coastline were "easier-going" than those living in inland city suburbs. True? Without reflecting on anyone's character I think the reason is both spiritual and obvious. To illustrate, the world-famous beach suburb of **Manly, N.S.W.** used to advertise itself as being **"Seven miles**

---

1   So-called "white" witches are more dangerous, in one sense, than "black" witches because they describe their abominations as "good" in the style of the serpent in the Garden of Eden.

from Sydney and a thousand miles from care". Going to work by ferry between Manly and Sydney was a daily experience of peace and serenity. How can one compare that with peak-hour traffic snarls, transport noises and exhaust fumes on the highways? **Oceanic water brings serenity.** Why? Because it is basically free from many types of spirits that attack mankind inwardly.

(iii) Websters International Dictionary defines **hydrotherapy** as the scientific treatment of disease by means of water. It is a scientific fact that water has a positive therapeutic effect for a variety of human ailments - even people under mental stress find relief from spiritual pressures by **sailing on ship cruises** to forget their troubles. It is very difficult to take your troubles with you when you are **enjoying a swim** on a summer's day on a Sydney beach. We feel so clean, so fresh, so free. We leave our pressures behind on the land. Most of us find that **taking a shower or a bath not only refreshes the body but the mind and soul also.**

(iv) I heard **Barry Smith** (the New Zealand prophet on the End – time) say in late 1980 that, although he did not understand it, there was something special, **something supernatural, about baptism by immersion,** and I believe he is right. There IS something especially powerful that happens *WITHIN* the new convert when they are buried in the waters of baptism. Whether you believe in the validity of baptism by full immersion or by sprinkling, there is no doubt in my mind that the drama which often surrounds baptism by full immersion is due to the *invisible deliverance* **from unclean spirits** within the human soul that often takes place. Dr. John Rockey (Ph.D. [Angelicum, Rome] D, Phil. [Oxon]) writes, "I had been 'sprinkled upon' in the Anglican Church at my first baptism shortly after birth. I was then re-baptised (reconditionally baptised) and "poured upon" in the

Catholic Church when I was three and a half years old. Yet, when about 45 years old, I felt distinctly directed by the Lord to be baptised by immersion in the Christian Life Centre (Pentecostal) pool. **The release was most noticeable!"**

The indwelling unclean spirits are terrified by full immersion and a considerable release from them is often experienced without the person being baptised realising what is happening. To them their baptism is a memorable occasion when God touched them and blessed them, but a major part of the blessing is that there is an exodus of the unclean from their souls.

Let us reflect on this for a moment. People receiving baptism by full immersion are usually dipped under the water by two brethren and their heads lifted out again very quickly, and they are usually gasping or breathing heavily for a few seconds. Why? Why the gasps?

It cannot be the cold water, because they have been standing in it for a few minutes beforehand, and in any event, the temperature of the water doesn't seem to be relevant because the same gasping takes place in warm water also.

It cannot be that they are short of breath because the dipping seldom takes more than TWO SECONDS. **It cannot be the shock of surprise** because the dipping is expected and there is plenty of warning.

What is it, then, that causes the gasping? It is the invisible deliverance that is taking place as unclean spirits panic and leave.

Why would demons flee at the prospect or experience of full immersion? Is it because the subject is appealing to God for a clean conscience (1 Peter 3:21) and the Holy Spirit is hovering nearby ready to seal the expectant heart into the Kingdom of God? Perhaps, but in that case **the same would also be true** of those who believe in the sufficiency of sprinkling water for baptism, and others who delay baptism. No, we need to look elsewhere for the full explanation, and I believe Peter's reference to the Great Flood of Noah's day as a type of baptism which put to death the old (earth), and cleansed it and Noah and his family, gives us the clue we are looking for (1 Peter 3:20-21).

When God destroyed the earth by flood, He cleansed it from incredible evil. Previously it was a demons picnic - except for Noah and his family. When the flood came it brought death to all flesh, and unclean spirits all over the face of the earth became discarnate (i.e. removed from bodies of flesh, bodiless) because they indwell the soul, and upon death the soul leaves the body. **For nearly twelve months (cf. Gen. 7:11 with 8:13)** the demons could not find a home because the waters covered the face of the earth. What a horrifying prospect for each "strong man" kicked out of his house (by death) and no future prospects in sight. **Their picnic turned to panic!** Not only was the flood a horrifying and dramatic judgement against human beings but it was equally disastrous for evil within the human beings. Demons have never forgotten the Flood, for in it they tasted the judgement of God upon themselves, and even though they know God does not intend to destroy the earth by water a second time, (Gen. 9:11, 2 Peter 3:6-7) baptism by full immersion in the name of our Lord Jesus Christ relives a nightmare for them.

Their Time is pre-ordained

Their task is to find another home. Legion indicates that this situation exists at least *until the Time of Torment (Judgement Day?)* when the spirit named Legion called out, **"Have you come here to torment us before the time?"** (Matt. 8:29). In other words, they have a dispensation of time which they roam with some measure of "freedom". Perhaps "freedom" is not the right word but they have an area of activity, a discretion, a modus operandi (until the Time of Torment) that is given them in the sovereign will of God and this is all part of the spiritual battle between Christ with the angels of God on the one side, and satan with his fallen angels on the other. So they are not supposed to be tormented before the Time, which I interpret as being their Judgement Day.

I read with interest that **Doreen Irvine** experienced the demons in herself putting up the same argument when she was receiving deliverance under the ministry of a Mr. Neil. She wrote, "They knew that if they were cast out to Gehenna (Hell) it would be the end of them. **'Not before the Time'** they would plead ... Many of the demons quoted scriptures, many argued over Bible truths..." [1]

WHERE to send them?

(a)   Legion argues vigorously **not to be sent out of the local country.** The word "country" here really means the local region, the region thereabouts, and not national boundaries as we sometimes understand it. If you send them ten miles you are sending them out of the country, and fifty miles is well out of the country as far as it means the local countryside, the region where they were used to running about in the creature they were in-dwelling.

Experience indicates that unclean spirits **hate being sent out of their local region** and that the fuss made by Legion in the biblical account appears to be how they normally feel about being dispatched some distance. When we understand this we can make three useful tactical comments about the warfare:

---

1   "From Witchcraft to Christ," pp.136-7.

(i) As satan is not omnipresent (he can't be everywhere at once), his kingdom is broken up into a network of rulers and authorities (kings and princes) which are commissioned by him to do certain tasks, and rule over allocated geographical areas. (Dan. 10:12-14, 20-21; Eph. 6:12) The whole world does indeed lie in the power of the evil one but he can only exercise that rule through delegating his somewhat dubious authority by chain of command, so that each and every one of us knows the temptations of the devil. However, when the deliverance minister despatches them outside the area commissioned to them by the local ruling spirit, he or she puts a spanner in the works. For rulers and authorities it means changed orders are necessary - a new deployment of forces available. **We Christians may not have the authority to send them into hell or hades or the abyss (which we will discuss in a moment) but we can certainly disrupt and disorganise the deployment of evil forces.** There is very little unity between unclean spirits and they only band together in warfare when they are forced to by desperate situations. They play the POWER (OVER OTHERS) GAME all the time, through us. As one would expect, **satan rules his kingdom of demons by fear, and they are all looking out for themselves.** A house or a kingdom divided against itself cannot stand, and when Jesus applied these words to the kingdom of satan He implied that demons share a unity in regard to the occupancy of God's creations, but that is about as far as their unity goes. There is an obvious sense in which satan's kingdom is united (in matters of occupancy and survival) and there is also a hidden sense in which his kingdom IS divided. I believe that Jesus was speaking in a mystery and in effect foretelling the eventual fall of that kingdom - and great will be the fall thereof. To the question: "How shall his (satan's) kingdom stand?" (Matt. 12:26). The answer is that it will NOT be able to stand - hallelujah!

(ii)   This characteristic of hating being sent out of the country gives the deliverance minister **an enormous weapon in obtaining obedience** from "disobedient" spirits. They are all disobedient, of course, but some are more tenacious in their disobedience than others. A threat to send them to the Indian Ocean, never to come within 100 miles of any shipping lanes or 'plane routes' is usually suffcient to hurry up those which are wasting your time. The prospect of being over water without hope of ever inhabiting a living creature again (except perhaps seagulls) until the Time, is horrifying to them. A lesser disciplinary measure may be to despatch them hundreds of miles - never to return. You can work it out for yourself, but make sure you are operating "in the Spirit".

(iii) It must be obvious that people who experience bad attacks of **home – sickness** MAY have a hidden SPIRITUAL cause. Home – sickness may be overcome (a) by **the human spirit asserting its own will,** or (b) by **the acceptance of the will of the indwelling Holy Spirit,** or (c) by the indwelling unclean spirit (if that is the cause) accepting a fresh commission from its new area ruler for its new environment, or, best of all (d) the breaking of the soul link and the REMOVAL of the unclean spirit.

(b)   **Legion asked to be sent into other animals,** the herd of swine, which request Jesus grants. (Mark 5:12-13, Matt. 8:31-32, Luke 8:32). However, for most situations today large numbers of unpopular, "unclean" animals (and it is very suitable, of course, that unclean spirits should go into "unclean" animals) are not likely to be available as substitute houses for unclean spirits when they are removed from a person. **There is no doubt that animals can be demonised** as both the Word of God and experience testify.

(c)   **Legion begs NOT to be commanded to depart into the Abyss.** It seems strange that on the strength of this verse, the

Abyss should be thought of as the abode of demons, as various Bible Dictionaries suggest. In fact, if that is their abode, they seem very reluctant to go there (Luke 8:31). You would think they would be happy to go to their abode, but that is not the case. Why? Because the abode they really want is (human) flesh.

Questions

Obviously Jesus could have sent Legion into the abyss (but didn't) so **the following questions are therefore raised:**

(i)	If Jesus could cast demons into the abyss, cannot we do the same? No. We do not have ALL AUTHORITY in Heaven and in earth, like Jesus.

(ii)	If demons could be *cast into the abyss (pit)* BY CHRISTIANS, **would not that render them harmless until the close of the Age?** If so, we have more problems, e.g. if we are able to despatch them into the abyss and render them entirely harmless, are we not able to *wipe out evil* before the Second Coming?

But that can't be right because things are to get worse, not better, according to the Bible - satan and his hosts are going to have their fling before Christ returns. What are we trying to do? You can see that we need to be careful here, that we understand the purpose and the history of the Bible and eschatology, that is, the teaching of the End Time or Last Things. We have to understand this carefully. **I don't believe we can render demons permanently harmless in this present dispensation.** I don't think we have the prerogative or authority to do so, from the Scriptures.

(iii)	Why did Jesus not cast them either out of the country or into the abyss? Why did He permit their question and let them go into the swine, where they wanted to go?

(iv) Does the request "Do not torment us before the Time" and the passage regarding wandering the waterless and dry places, imply that demons are to have a "free" reign until Judgement in order to try the nations and the hearts of the people? - (excepting of course that they can be expelled from the Children of God). We know that many people become Children of God because they are troubled by demons and they know they need help. Constantly people are coming forward who are unconverted and who are prepared to receive Christ because their needs are so great, and the spiritual battle is very real to them. Let us now look for some answers!

Regarding the first question above, can Christians cast demons into the abyss? Let us have a closer look at what the Bible says about the abyss. The Book of Revelation gives us most of the information, but I am going to stick my neck out and say that I am not aware of any suggestion in the scriptures that Christians can despatch demons there, before the Time.

The word "abyss" means literally "boundless, bottomless" and in the Old Testament is usually translated "the deep". (Gen. 1:2, Isa. 44:27, Job 38:16, 41:32)

Paul describes the abyss as the place of the underworld or the abode of the DEAD (Rom. 10:7) while Revelation simply tells us that there is an Angel of the abyss who holds its key (Rev. 9:1–2) whose name is Abaddon (destruction) or Apollyon (destroyer–Rev. 9:11) and that satan will be locked up there 1000 years (Rev. 20:1–3). From it, locusts (symbolic of demons?) plague the pagan earth (Rev. 9:3–10) but **nowhere is there any suggestion that a Christian man can despatch demons there.** The abyss belongs to a largely unknown area of God's purposes and whereas the demons were momentarily frightened that Jesus would send them into the abyss for torment before their appointed time, *He did not.* He did not torment before the time for, I suggest, to do so would have confused dispensations or epochs. **Their time for torment or**

the abyss has not yet come.

My conclusion is therefore that *this is one area where Christians can not do what Jesus could have done.* He ALONE can break dispensations, rules and times which are known only within the secret will of the Godhead. We who are sons of God by adoption and grace only have the authority now **in matters revealed by God's Word** and which are within the New Testament dispensation. That is to say, until the Lord returns. **Our authority is that which the New Testament gives us.** We should not go beyond or exceed that authority and therefore we have no authority to send demons into the abyss YET, because **demons must continue in the divine will and purpose of God to sort out the hearts of men and women across the face of the earth**. It seems to me that they are going to be more active than ever during the Great Tribulation soon to come. Alternatively, *the Tribulation will come to nothing if the Christian church can dispose of all the demons around the world before the time, and against the revealed will of God in the New Testament.* We will judge them eventually (1 Cor 6:3).

Summary

There is no authority that I can see for sending demons to the place of departed spirits or hades or Gehenna (hell) etc. for precisely the same reasons as there is no authority for sending them to the abyss or pit. **These notions are purely religious and romantic fantasies** and there are no grounds for them in the New Testament. We have authority to cast them (1) out and away, perhaps (2) out of the country and (3) never to return, but as far as sending them to "unknown" or exotic places outside of this planet earth, I see no authority for that in the scriptures; and I certainly do NOT recommend taking any unauthorised course that will buy an argument with demons and give them an excuse to prolong the battle.

5. 5 TRANSFERENCE OF SPIRITS

(i) BEWARE DURING MINISTRY.

The whole question of transference is one of HOW did we become demonised? We touch on this again in the following chapters[1] under "CAUSES" but it is helpful to discuss this subject here, in the context of ministry to sufferers.

So far we have discussed where to send demons, and certain places where, in my opinion, we have no authority to send them, but we ought not to close this section without a reminder that unclean spirits that are being cast out are always on the lookout for an opportunity to transfer into nearby Christians, especially those ministering. They know they are being removed, so if they find a minister lax in his spiritual concentration and ministering "in the flesh" without taking up his spiritual weapons and safeguards (of covering with the Blood, binding, etc.),[2] then a transference into the minister would turn defeat into victory for them. But do not be alarmed - the Shield of Faith will quench all their evil plans. **Just remember not to underestimate the enemy and be prepared for anything.** When the enemy sees this, he is far less likely to cause you problems.

(ii) BEWARE AT DEATH

(a) Approaching Death[3]

Demons are not only eager to transfer at ministry time but also when death is approaching. They need a body to inhabit through which they can manifest their unclean personalities and perform unclean deeds. Consequently **when death is approaching they are very alert to the prospect of finding a new home in any passer-by.** Demons do not necessarily

1   Chapter 7, Book 3

2   See Chapter 3, Book 1

3   Here we refer to the EXPERIENCE of death, the SPIRIT of death is discussed in Book 4.

wait for death to take place but will leave days or weeks beforehand if they believe that death is likely. Coughing and vomiting may not only be due to the removal of physical poisons but may also be the departure of spirits for any number of reasons. To illustrate, an elderly person goes to hospital and their prognosis is not good. They sit up in their hospital bed - their eyes are "wild" or fearful or strangely blank - not at all like they usually are. You visit them and they see you while you are still metres away, and the fear in their eyes remains. You talk with them for a period and you notice they watch *everyone* who comes within visibility of the bed - not a person can walk nearby without coming under the concentrated scrutiny of those strange or fearful eyes. Why? Are they looking for help? Yes, but not the help you think. They are not looking for medical help or spiritual help - that spirit of fear in their eyes comes from the demons knowing that very soon they are going to have to find a new home, and **everyone who passes by is examined with a view to achieving a successful transference** into new homes, which are usually already infected with similar kingdoms of darkness to some extent.

(b) Death

It goes without saying that any unclean spirit that is unsuccessful in transferring into a "suitable" new body PRIOR to death will be **extremely active at the TIME of death** because it MUST then leave its old home anyway, and will become desperate for a new dwelling.

I never cease to be amazed at the parallels that exist between the visible creation and the spiritual world. For example, the experience of the **caterpillar** that lives a short life, falls asleep in a cocoon and then breaks out of its "grave" and flies away as a beautiful new creature, symbolises to me the life, death and resurrection of a Christian. An **iceberg** speaks to me of sin and death. It looks harmless, even beautiful, but in fact is very dangerous, with only a small fraction of its real size visible at any time, and it is as cold as death.

The other day a **blowfly** entered my bedroom and began to make a nuisance of itself. Failing to drive it out again, I resorted to fly-spray and because I caught it on a white curtain, I was able to observe the expelling or disgorging of many maggots or worms from its body as it died. Ugh! But it gave me an illustration of what happens in the spiritual realm when a living body experiences death, and unclean spirits are forced to leave.

(c) After Death

The Bible also seems to indicate that this **spiritual hyperactivity around a corpse may last for seven (7) days AFTER death:**

"He who touches the dead body of any man shall be unclean seven (7) days". (Numbers 19:11)

"... everyone that comes into the tent shall be unclean seven (7) days". (Numbers. 19:14)

If we first allow for the usual three (3) days after death and before burial, it would seem that the contamination period could be as much as ten (10) days after death occurs. I understand this to mean that the **unclean spirits expelled from the dead person's soul may hang around the scene of death for up to ten (10) days,** looking for similar new homes to transfer into, before scattering farther afield.

The remainder of Numbers 19 describes the methods to be used for de-contamination (purifying) of those affected and infected, but of course this need not alarm Christians because Christ has fulfilled the Old Testament solution of sin-offering (v.17); indeed ALL the *religious* Law.

What we Christians need to do now is to RECEIVE THE WARNING from Numbers 19 and MAKE SURE WE APPLY THE NEW TESTAMENT WEAPONS given us through the

Blood of Christ,[1] especially when we find ourselves in situations where death is approaching, or has taken place.

Christians should ALWAYS live their lives under the covering of the Blood of the Passover Lamb for protection, and this is especially so for Christians in the medical profession, as well as the Clergy and regular hospital visitors. Non-Christians? They had better act quickly by repenting and getting converted - fast! - or suffer the consequences of being vulnerable to the powers of darkness.

iii) BEWARE WHEN COUNSELLING.

Anyone who is in a position where they are called upon to minister to the emotionally unstable or the mentally infirm is subject to spiritual attack. It ought not to surprise us that **psychiatrists** who are subject to daily manifestations from their patients should be particularly vulnerable to transference, and I do not think that many psychiatrists - even Christian psychiatrists - know how to protect themselves in **what is in reality spiritual warfare.**

One psychiatrist rang to ask me for help because he suddenly found himself conducting himself in a violent way towards his wife. This alarmed them both, but although they acknowledged that his change in behaviour was due to the dangerous nature of his work, we were unable to minister the blessings and protection of the Lord Jesus Christ to him, due to his unbelief.

Perhaps without his wife's hostility against placing his faith in the Lord Jesus, he might have come through into the Kingdom of God, and then receive the benefits (including deliverance) of being a member of that Kingdom, but, sadly, he did not.

Ministering and counselling the needy is spiritually dangerous work, as **the high casualty rate amongst counsellors (including suicide)** confirms. Knowing what I know now, I would not like to be involved in any such counselling or ministry

---

1   See Chapter 3, Book 1.

situation without knowing that I was protected and fully armed with the spiritual weapons available to me from the Lord Jesus.

(iv) BEWARE OF PHYSICAL AND SPIRITUAL INFECTION

We don't like people coughing or sneezing into our faces or over our food because of fear of infection from germs, but that is only the PHYSICAL reason. Christians ought always to be aware of the SPIRITUAL situation and claim **the protection of the Blood of the Passover Lamb,** using their **authority to bind and to loose,** and to **rebuke in Jesus' Name.** There is no need for alarm in any of these situations if the Lord's protection and authority has been properly applied.

(v) BEWARE OF OCCULT DEMONSTRATIONS.

Regardless of your Christian precautions, do not even be remotely involved in the abominable practices of anti-christ[1] whatever your motives, **except to come against them in Jesus' Name.** This includes watching demonstrations in films and television shows. Just as the Holy Spirit moving through Christian television Crusades etc. can bring you a blessing, so also **an unclean spirit can use a communications medium to pollute you, if you get involved.**

5. 6 COUNTING NUMBERS OF DEMONS

This is helpful only for the purposes of accurate recording, so that witness can be made truthfully to the saving power of Christ. For this purpose, that careful recorder and author, Luke, notes specifically that Jesus' cast out of Mary Magdalene SEVEN demons (Luke 8:2, see also Mark 16:9), in the Holy Scriptures; and even in Jesus' clash with Legion we gain the impression from the name 'Legion' that 4000 to 6000 demons were involved, as that was the approximate number of Roman

---

1   As the typescript of this book was in its final stages of preparation, I came across "The Devil's Alphabet" by Dr. Kurt Koch. He describes at least fifteen examples of transference in the context of death, counselling, infirmity, occult and sexual activity (pp. 111-119).

soldiers to a Roman Legion. But of course, every unclean empire in a human wants to grow bigger and stronger and **there is no way that the ruling spirit of Legion would have confined himself to only 6000** if he could increase to 106,000, simply because of his name "Legion". Therefore Legion may simply be a name reflecting an earlier situation when 6000 occupied or entered the man at a point in time, and may not have any bearing on the total number resident in the man when confronted by Jesus, except to indicate that thousands were involved.

Through the experience of our deliverance ministry I have been forced to consider another possibility which may seem "way-out" to the natural mind. I now believe that **each of the seven demons numbered in Mary Magdalene represents a demonic kingdom of hundreds of demons,** each headed by a ruling spirit – seven rulers in all. We already know that satan has a kingdom in human beings (Matt. 12:22, 25-29, 43-45; Eph. 2:1-3, 6:12; James 3:14-15).

The incident of the deliverance of the blind and dumb demoniac specifically teaches us that the removal of blind and dumb spirits by the Lord is the Kingdom of God displacing the kingdom of satan (Matt. 12:22-29) while **sin and death themselves are described as kings,** because although they reign **over unbelievers** they should not continue to reign or have dominion **over believers.** Christ has now become the King of their lives and HE should be reigning within (Rom. 5:12;14,17,21).

Therefore spirits of blindness and dumbness in the demoniac may be described as either:

(i) PART of the total kingdom of satan within the sufferer, known by the blanket term SIN,

OR

(ii) a separate **kingdom of blindness** and a separate

kingdom of dumbness operating under the **ruling strongman spirit,** i.e. small kings (rulers) and kingdoms operating under more powerful kings in the manner that Saxon kings ruled their local areas under Norman the Conqueror or that native kings in the British Commonwealth ruled their tribes but gave allegiance to the Sovereigns of England earlier this century. These are, of course, rough illustrations of the unclean spiritual network within the human soul, and which come under the blanket title of SIN.[1]

Now if this principle of numbering RULING SPIRITS ONLY is correct and applied consistently we should consider the possibility that LEGION CONSISTED OF AT LEAST 4000 TO 6000 RULERS, with hordes of minor spirits not worth mentioning. Certainly there is an interesting interchange from **singular** to **plural** by the spirit(s) named Legion.

> **"My name is Legion, for WE are many" (Mark 5:9).**
> **"What have I to do with you Jesus ... do not torment ME" (Mark 5:7).**
> **"What have WE to do with you ... have you come to torment US ..." (Matt. 8:29).**

Mark uses the term "unclean spirit" both in the singular and in the plural in this incident and Luke uses the word "demon" in both the singular and plural. This switching between singular and plural may best be illustrated from Mark.

> **"And he (the unclean spirit) begged Him (Jesus) eagerly not to send THEM out of the country (v 10) ... and THEY begged Him ..." (V 12).**

Clearly **a single spirit may represent many spirits or demons** and when we consider the horrible mess that is presented to us as Legion's character[2] (violent, fierce, defiling,

---

1   We expect to say more about SIN and ministering against kingdoms in Book 4
2   See Chapter 5.3 (iii).

suicidal, destructive, idolatrous, occult, swinish etc. etc.) it should not surprise us that what was in him could easily take over two thousand (2000) swine in sufficient numerical strength to lead them all to their destruction (Mark 5:13). This suggests to me that **each swine would have received at least two or three RULERS and AUTHORITIES, as** it is unlikely that weaker class spirits could have immediately caused such blind self-destruction. Even brute animals have a strong sense of self-preservation.

To put it more plainly, a Legion of 4000 spirits transferring into 2000 swine approximates 2 unclean spirits to each animal. Similarly a Legion of 6000 spirits transferring into 2000 swine approximates 3 unclean spirits to each animal. As these ALL came from the man with the LEGION, it follows that he would have carried thousands of RULER-class spirits!

If you are prone to dismiss this out of hand as incredible or unbelievable it might help to consider how many dangerous bacteria we now know live within a normal person's human body, and remind ourselves that science itself has proved what was once ludicrous, and what is possible in the natural world is even more possible in the SPIRITUAL.

The fact remains that the evil powers in the man with the Legion were strong enough to lead 2000 swine to self-destruct. The explanation I offer is no more incredible than that.

If this spiritual concept is true, and I believe it is, it would explain why sufferers thought of as **psychiatric cases need so much ministry and help through a continuous program,** until such time as we ministers can minister at the level of Jesus' anointing and ministry to the man with the Legion. However if you find this concept unacceptable please do not allow it to prejudice your overall view of the ministry, but take what you can receive and build your ministry on the basics. The truth or otherwise of what I am saying here will be revealed soon enough.

So far we have approved the counting of demons (kingdoms?) only for the purposes of truthful testimony, and there should be no other motive for counting demons, except perhaps to expose their widespread prevalence. I am of the opinion that, with the development of powerful anointed ministries of deliverance in these last days, unclean spirits will sometimes pour out of sufferers like a torrent, and counting may well be impracticable, if not impossible.

5. 7 WHAT ABOUT THE DRAMA?

(i) MANIFESTATIONS.

We have said a little about this already[1] - Manifestations are simply a "showing forth". Whenever we sin - we manifest sin, when we are greedy - we manifest greed, when we are angry - we manifest anger. We can either manifest **the works of the flesh** or **the fruit of the Spirit** (Gal. 5:19-23) and the two kingdoms (God's and satan's) constantly seek to manifest themselves through us. Many unclean spirits can only manifest their character and nature through flesh. They have no arms or legs as such, so they need arms and legs of flesh with which to carry out their evil deeds and manifest themselves. When we see a good friend acting strangely out-of-character, we say to him, "What's got into you?" - and there is more truth in our question than perhaps we realise at the time. So in the normal course of everyday life, unclean spirits manifest themselves through sinful, unclean behaviour or speech (e.g. profanity and blasphemy).

When we come to the ministry of deliverance, we have a situation where unclean spirits may try NOT to manifest or give themselves away. It becomes a deadly "game" of hide-and-seek. However, after you have commanded them to manifest and depart to their appointed place in Jesus' Name, this they must begin to do, sometimes quietly and unobtrusively, sometimes with varying degrees of drama. Remember that

---

1   Book 1, Chapter 1, pages 5-8.

they are unclean breaths[1] and they may simply pass out through the body without any obvious manifestation at all; but the majority will look for a flesh exit such as the mouth, nose, ears and anus; so coughing, yawning, burping, sneezing, retching, crying and wailing will be fairly normal forms of manifestations by departing spirits. The more difficult departures to pick up will be those leaving through the hands and feet, and the top of the head, but in such cases the subject usually "feels" activity in those areas, and sometimes continuing aches and pains. However, such symptoms are a cause for praise, NOT alarm.

I remember the case of a man being ministered to for involvement with the occult and he began to complain of pain in the back of the neck. He refused to continue with ministry, proclaiming that God doesn't cause pain when He heals or delivers people. Well, of course, that is true - God doesn't, but when the powers of darkness are being removed or expelled in what a Sydney psychiatrist once called **"spiritual surgery"**, they are literally being torn out of the soul - out of the bones (marrow) and the blood stream (Levit. 17:11-12,14) - by the ministry of the Holy Spirit, and this can cause some discomfort to the sufferer. It is the powers of darkness being removed, roots and tentacles, that causes the discomfort - not the Holy Spirit of God. One has only to study the deliverance of the epileptic boy who was deaf and dumb (Mark 9:20,26) to understand this.

The pain may be an attempt to "put off" the subject from proceeding, as is any other discomfort, but the Lord is good, and I cannot remember this ploy being successful more than a few times during more than twenty years of ministry (1 Cor. 10:13).

Sniffly noses usually means that exit is being used, as is the case with watery and stinging eyes. Leg pains, usually from within the bones, are very common during successful ministry,

1   Book 1, chapter 1, pages 5 – 6.

and it is important that the sufferer assist as much as possible by **keeping their spirit focused on Jesus,** usually through the singing of praise, and NOT on their symptoms or manifestations.

Most manifestations will mean that the commands given in Jesus' Name are being obeyed. Just one word of caution here. **Some noisy spirits may attempt to deceive you.** They try to stay by giving the impression they are going - discernment and sensitivity to the leading of the Holy Spirit is necessary in such cases. Noisy manifestations which are not an integral part of successful ministry are utterly worthless; indeed, they are disruptive and deceptive rather than profitable. It is up to the minister of the Lord to control the situation and get victory.

(ii) ACCEPTABLE DRAMA

The Christian who is ministering should be in *control* of the situation by exercising Godly authority in Jesus' Name. However, **there can be drama from time to time as** revealed in the Scriptures, viz:

"And the unclean spirit CONVULSING him, and CRYING with a LOUD voice, came out of him". (Mark 1:26) (see also Acts 8:7)

To this incident Luke adds: "And when the demon had THROWN HIM DOWN in the midst ..." (Luke 4:35)

Also the following are helpful -

"And whenever it seizes him, it dashes him down (TEARS HIM) and he foams and grinds his teeth and becomes rigid ..." (Mark 9:18)

"And when the spirit saw him (Jesus) immediately it CONVULSED the boy, and he FELL on the ground, and ROLLED about FOAMING ..." (Mark 9:20) (also Luke 9:39-42)

Any Christian who finds these kind of scenes too horrible or dramatic to stomach, or lacking in refinement or respectability, or in conflict with their idea of good order and decency, ought to forget about this ministry entirely and stick to something safe and respectable (to men). I only ask that if it's not YOUR "cup-of-tea", **please don't criticise** or **hinder** those who have the courage and conviction to minister in Jesus' Name to those who need this kind of deliverance. Be supportive and do whatever lies within your capacity, gifts and abilities in Christ to help.

If Jesus had dramatic incidents during His ministry, then we might reasonably expect the same, It is not necessarily lack of control because Christ was in control of every situation, but it just simply means that *sometimes* there are some dramatics before something disappears, and we must expect that.

Dramatic deliverance used to be quite a common occurrence at our meetings but since the Lord provided the Power of God in ever–increasing measure (see next section) things have quietened down considerably–praise His Holy Name!

(iii) UNACCEPTABLE DRAMA

Violent behaviour by the sufferers to themselves, the counsellors or anyone at all **is totally unacceptable,** and if this should take place it means that the minister(s) have temporarily lost control of the situation. In the early days of the ministry, before I received ministry myself, I found myself in a number of situations which were potentially violent and from which the Lord has taught me **how to keep control, and regain control** where that became necessary.

There is nothing new or profound in this. It is simply a matter of exercising AUTHORITY and POWER. Most Christians know this in THEORY; they may even be taught it in Bible College - but **it is more than that**. When an unclean spirit resisted the ministry and threatened me with personal bodily harm in the early days of my training, I used to minister authoritatively with varying degrees of desperation, but NOW such opposition **brings a welling up of RIGHTEOUS indignation and anger from within me.** How dare these foul things threaten a servant and a son of the Most High God? Today, I not only know my authority in Christ in THEORY, but I FEEL it and KNOW it in the inner man. I experience it throughout my being as I use it. It is as if Jesus has taken me over totally and they are disobeying Him - not little me!

While the Lord protected me in some incredibly dangerous situations from the beginning, nevertheless He allowed me to experience some violence in order to teach me to avoid **over-confidence** which leads to **cocksureness** and **pride** which leads to **presumption** - which leads to loss of spiritual concentration or awareness in the spirit, all of which can lead to setbacks, which are serious from the sufferer's point of view.

The alcoholic

I once brought an alcoholic into the church vestry one Saturday. He rang the door-bell and I immediately knew it was an alcoholic because they nearly always lean on the bell for at least ten seconds before they ease off it again. To make a long story short - I brought him into the house and he challenged me aggressively and said, "What is all this exorcism business I saw in the newspapers?" And I said, "Yes, Tom, what do you want to know?" He said. "Well, if it is right, come on, come on". And I said, "You have to have faith, Tom; you have to have faith in Christ". "I've got faith in Christ, I've got faith in Christ" he insisted. So, I brought him into the vestry and he was one of those poor fellows with atrophied nerves in the legs. You know how alcoholics sometimes lose control of their legs and can't walk normally. He shuffled in and I sat him down. With an alcoholic you almost always have to have a bucket handy, and sure enough he started to retch into the bucket as soon as the ministry began.

Then we seemed to strike a period where there was a block, and then he said, "I don't believe all this", which was really the clue I needed. So I started to sing choruses of *faith* around him. He was sitting on the chair and glared up at me because he didn't have the legs to get up and attack me, although he tried. He said, "I don't believe, I don't believe!" So when I commanded the spirit of unbelief - ugh! - it all came out. Yet it was really beautiful. The ministry continued and he tried to get up to attack me again but could not, and all this was going on while I was enjoying myself with the Lord, just out of arm's reach, singing choruses. This incident may give you some idea of what might have happened if he could have used his legs.

A slap on the face

On another occasion I was ministering to a young lady together with lady counsellors and she was just sitting quietly when suddenly - Whack! - right across the face! The shock stunned me for a short moment although I was unhurt (Luke 10:19), and then it was back with the ministry harder than ever, but more warily. She said, "Oh, I"m terribly sorry, I didn't mean to do that; it wasn't me". I'm sure the Lord permitted it to teach me, and to teach *you*!

More recently, since my wife Verlie has taken on the role of Deliverance Minister, there was an incident where she was ministering powerfully and standing close to a group of sufferers seated on chairs.

I noticed one man's eyes begin to glint fiercely at her and was about to warn her to keep clear of him when he rose with a roar and raised his hands to strike her. His arms flailed, briefly, because some invisible force immediately flattened him to the ground and he was completely "out" for the rest of the meeting.

"He" only succeeded in making contact with Verlie by the barest touch. The angel of the Lord did just enough to protect Verlie without harming the brother in any way.

Indeed, he received a wonderful release. As for Verlie, she took it all in her nonchalant stride and continued ministering.

A Show for a Bishop

There will always be a number of cases from which satan tries to take advantage and tear down the ministry by playing on the ignorance of the world and the Church. In the early days a Bishop visited a session of our group deliverance and one young lady stood up and threw a flurry of punches at me - for only one reason. The demons in her were grandstanding and hoping to influence him into reporting adversely on the ministry. They needn't have bothered - he wasn't impressed with them - in fact, he wasn't impressed with anything! Another young man, full of destruction, became incredibly strong when manifesting destruction, and broke the back of a church pew with his own back muscles (no hands), and I was unwise enough to tell another Bishop who knew that the same thing had happened at the preaching of Berridge in the year 1759, viz:

> "And such were the mysterious phenomena which came to light under the preaching of Berridge all through that first summer, though he never played on the taut feelings of his hearers for the purpose nor set any great store by such signs when they did appear. **Sometimes men would struggle in such anguish of mind that the very pews were broken;** sometimes they would sit through all that they had heard as if unaffected, and then drop on their way home. They would fall down like dead men and lie where they fell, on the road, or in his garden, for they could not even walk the short two hundred yard path from the church to his house. Both Wesley and Berridge watched it all at the time with a sense of awe and caution, but we need not now feel concerned either to defend or explain these things; they passed away in course of time, but they were a sign to many that God was there in power both to wound and to heal".[1]

---

1   "Cambridge and the Evangelical Succession" pp. 77-78, by Marcuš Loane.

"HOW DID THE EXORCISM GO?"

Acknowledgements to "London Express News and Feature Services" for permission to use this HAROLD BREDE cartoon.

A woman with eastern religious spirits manifested aggressively and had to be held firmly by four counsellors while she was being cleansed. Later her husband noticed bruises on her arms where she had been firmly held, and took her in to be interviewed by yet another Bishop who was understandably very sympathetic and "tut tutted" appropriately. **I was fast running out of friends on the board of Bishops!** Looking back I can see that **it was all part of an orchestrated attack upon the ministry.** When I told the other counsellors how satan was trying to put the ministry down, they were incensed with righteous indignation and said, "If they think ... was bruised, they should take a look at us!" They were understandably upset briefly, but we were learning how satan plays on the fears and widespread lack of understanding of the deliverance ministry and **manipulates even Blood-bought Christians,** the more senior the better!

5.8 THE POWER OF GOD

(i) THE LORD'S ANSWER TO DRAMA.

All these illustrations of violence come from the early days of the ministry, up to 1976, and this problem of violence was soon attended to by the Lord when He gave our most gifted and anointed minister at that time, what is known as *the Power of God* in large measure. When the Holy Spirit renders someone "under the power" it is as if they lose the power of their flesh to stand in His presence and they fall to the ground, *conscious but basically powerless* in God's hand, as experienced under the preaching of Berridge in the 18th century.

I had prayed long and hard to the Lord for this provision of God's power without actually realising what I was praying for.

The prayers were born of desperation because St. Michael's Church Hall is located in a highly residential area of the inner City of Sydney, and every time a Deliverance Meeting was held the unclean spirits made an enormous racket (noise - hullabaloo - din) as they were leaving.

The hall was turned into a veritable mad–house, similar to that experienced by the Wesleyan reformers of 200 years ago. Screams, yells, growls weeping and roaring had me praying desperately in two ways:

(i)   that the Lord would put his "blanket" over the building and let none of the sounds be heard outside.

(ii)   that the Lord would deafen the local residents so that there would be no complaints and no visits from the police, shutting us down.

The Lord heard my cry and answered in a way I did not expect; in a way that took care of the neighbours, but even more importantly, cared for the sufferers as well. He supplied "the Power of God".

Sometimes a strong spirit may emerge and manifest dramatically even when the sufferer is under the power of God on the floor or carpet. In the early days I would signal the counsellors to assist me by holding down the sufferer so that the thrashing about did not cause them to injure themselves against walls or furniture, but with the level of the Power of God we now have during ministry **I prefer to leave the sufferer un-held by human hands.** We put such cases well away from physical obstacles and let them thrash (a little), while under the watchful eye of a counsellor. Should a strong spirit manifest in a person who is located close to obstacles I ask a counsellor or put myself between the sufferer and the obstacle so that any physical restraining is only applied as a last resort.

It is better to let them squirm about, and rather remove the furniture if necessary, exercising control by your voice in Jesus' Name, and commanding them to come out QUICKLY and QUIETLY and HARMLESSLY.

There is no question that some demons are exhibitionists and the Power of God is a great help in quelling disturbances. Drama should not be encouraged but may eventuate and should not cause alarm provided you have a good grasp of your Christian authority over the principalities and powers, and you are exercising God's anointed calling to the work. Do not be unnerved when some demons wail "the wail of defeat" as they leave, but rejoice.

Laying-on-of-hands

Neither Verlie nor I lay on hands unless led by the Lord but I would have to say that during emergency one-to-one or small group ministry we usually are led to lay on hands from time to time.

Sometimes the unclean spirit in the sufferer will push your hand(s) away and in such circumstances I normally press on with the laying-on-of-hands, instructing counsellors to gently restrain the sufferer's arm actions. So if the unclean spirit is panicking and resisting because of the laying-on-of-hands that suits me fine and I usually continue with it.

Dangerous situations

A man walked in off the street and into my Church and said, "Minister to me or I'm going to kill someone". He was full of murder and hate. We rang the police and they obligingly kept themselves handy outside the Church (unbeknown to him) while we proceeded to minister - first the power of God and secondly the ministry of deliverance. I believe the Lord saved two lives that Saturday afternoon - the visitor's and the person he hated and was bent on killing. There was an element of risk humanly speaking, but we really had no choice and, praise God, he was thoroughly defused. He came in like a lion and went out like a lamb - Praise the Name of the Lord! There was no time for counselling or psychiatrists (we tried to contact his psychiatrist without success) and so we were thrown TOTALLY on the Lord, and in this instance *the Power of God was absolutely vital in minimising the physical side of the ministry.* It sickens me when deliverance ministers are blamed for causing deaths - such ignorance - but that is satan's favourite ploy. By the grace of God you could save 99 suicidal or destructive people out of 100, and the one you lose (through no fault of your own) may be taken and used in evidence against you to destroy you. Do you still want to be a deliverance minister? - the 99 make it worth it! And though many may be ignorant, God is not!

On the great Day of the Lord you will stand justified in His presence, while your enemies shall be ashamed.

God is our defence

Deliverance ministers are VULNERABLE and dependent on the Lord and His Holy Word in a way NO OTHER Christian is vulnerable and dependent. Every time you minister you stick your neck out a long way for the Lord, and satan is just itching to chop it off - he has plenty of people who'll do the job for him, especially "mature" Christians, who know just enough to be unhelpful and negative.

Beware of the demons of **destruction.** They are fairly prevalent in **occult** and **religious** cases and invariably go together with **hatred, karate, alcoholic** and **homosexual** spirits. It is especially with spirits such as these that some sedation between sessions, and under the eye of a spiritually-aware Christian medical practitioner, *may* be wise (unless you are greatly anointed with power) depending on the strength of the spirits you face. **Ideally** the deliverance minister should look for total deliverance of the **destructive sufferer** in one session so that nothing remains in their soul to cause trouble in the future. However, where this ideal is not possible because of the time factor (and it rarely is), the second best arrangement may be to have the sufferer remain under *informed* Christian psychiatric care so that a life of moderation and harmlessness can be lived in-between deliverance sessions. Drugs should be kept to a minimum (remembering that ministry will probably be necessary for drug-damage side-effects later) and normally should not be taken prior to ministry as the deliverance minister will want to attack the

NORMAL afflicted condition of the subject - not a medicated condition, *as far as this is practical.* However, no RISKS should be taken. **Presumption is neither faith nor wisdom.**

Church hospitals?

It will be interesting to see whether any of the major church denominations which have established church hospitals will ever have the vision to set aside (say) one wing of each of their hospital properties to provide professional nursing and accommodation for people receiving deliverance from demonisation, plus a comfortable sound-proofed and padded deliverance room where choruses of praise and the reading of the scriptures can be ministered continuously through a P.A. system or cassette player in assistance to the deliverance ministries conducted. In such places the heaviest dramas could be enacted safely and in perfect privacy, and they could also supply the ongoing 24-hours-a-day care necessary for speedy cleansing and renewal of each and every precious child of God. Pray that the Lord will raise up courageous reformers like Luther, Calvin, Wesley and Ryle to lead and inspire God's people again, for their needs TODAY, and Church properties be used for the cleansing and healing of SOULS!

I have no doubt that the results would compare so favorably with those obtained by medical methods in Government hospitals as to cause a major upheaval and revolutionise the attitudes of people from all walks of life, so that the Name of the Lord Jesus Christ would be extolled throughout the land.

However for this to happen it will be necessary for some Churches to break free of the religious spirits that control them, and enter into the fulness of the HOLY SPIRIT.

Healing and deliverance

As we have already indicated in the previous section, the Power of God reduces the hazards of ministry for both the sufferer and the minister. In examining this subject we especially want to focus on that part of the Holy Spirit's activities which heals, casts out demons and removes from humans the ability to stand on their legs, and thus brings them to the ground - literally. Obviously if we were to study the power of God in ALL its manifestations, it would be necessary to study the complete works of the Holy Spirit, for where the Holy Spirit is, there is the Power of God! So then, our emphasis in this brief study is on the manifestation of the power of God which **heals, casts out demons and causes people to fall to the ground.**

In the early 1960's a Christian neighbour told me how she had gone forward during a service at a general invitation to those who desired special prayer. When the Pastor prayed for her, she fell over backwards because of some invisible power, but was unhurt because the incident was anticipated and someone was behind her to catch and lower her to the floor. She remained conscious and able to hear and see everything around her clearly, but was somewhat limited in her movements, she said. Knowing the witness as completely trustworthy, I was mystified and intrigued. If this was of God, what good did it do? - I asked myself. At that time this experience was also being called "slain in the Spirit" which made me even more uneasy.

Many years later, in 1974, I discovered that this experience was a regular and important feature of the ministry of many ministers, and I gained at least ONE answer to the question of its value. It quickly became invaluable in the deliverance and healing ministries growing at that time, in a way which we shall see.

(ii) THE MINISTRY OF JESUS

When we look at the scripture, the most obvious thing that stands out is that deliverance and healing require POWER so that the Jews ask, **"Where did this man ... get these powerful works?"** (Matt. 13:54), and Dr. Luke testifies that **"the power of the Lord was in Him (Jesus) to heal (cure)"**

(Luke 5:17).

This power is apparently of a quality that can be FELT or experienced in the flesh because Jesus perceived **"that power had gone forth from Him"** (Mark 5:30) in the healing of the woman with the issue of blood, and others who touched his garments were healed also (Mark 6:56), apparently in the same way. The healed also felt the power in their flesh (Mark 5:29).

It is NOT physical but spiritual, yet it can be felt IN or THROUGH the flesh.

Perhaps a less obvious use of the power of God by Jesus, but more closely related to our enquiry, is the deliverance of the **deaf, dumb and epileptic boy:**

> "And after crying out and convulsing him terribly, it came out and **the boy was like a corpse** so that many said, **'He is dead.'** But Jesus took him by the hand and lifted him and he stood up". (Mark 9:25-26)

There are only a few incidents of deliverance in the Bible that are recorded in any significant detail (e.g. Legion), while there are numerous references to this ministry in general narrative. This should indicate to us that we give the *closest attention to the DETAILED texts concerning deliverance as KEYS that unlock the more general information* about the ministry.

In the incident (above) the boy is convulsed (no doubt horrifying the bystanders), the demon is expelled and the boy **"was as dead"** so that many said, **"He is dead!"** This, of course, is a classical description of people who are receiving deliverance or healing while under the power of God. They often appear "as dead" and therefore it is not surprising that the Holy Spirit should follow much the same pattern for ministry today.

Two further scriptures about Jesus' ministry are worth looking at:

> "When He said to them, **'I am'**, they drew back and FELL on the ground". (John 18:6)

> "When I saw Him, I FELL at His feet AS DEAD. And He placed His right hand on me saying, 'Fear not, I am the first and the last ...'" (Rev. 1:17)

The quotation from John's Gospel is in the context of Jesus' seizure in the Garden of Gethsemane. The falling to the ground of the mob is usually explained by their horror at the use of the words **"I am"**, which are supposed to be unutterable for devout Jews, being the words of identification of God in Exodus 3:14 **"You shall say to the children of Israel, I AM has sent me to you"**. Certainly Jesus' answer evoked a murderous reaction in a previous clash (John 8:58-59) but not so when used by the man born blind (John 9:9); so I feel this explanation is somewhat unsatisfactory. In any event the incident suggests a united reaction of *COMPULSIVE* character by the mob rather than a premeditated or ritualistic reaction (such as rending garments) and I believe that they were thrown to the ground by the Power of God. It proves nothing by itself but is worth noting in the light of other similar incidents - for example, the apostle John's experience when given the Revelation. In Chapter One, John is "in the Spirit" (v. 10) and has a vision of the Living One (vv. 13- 18) the appearance of whom causes John to FALL AS DEAD at HIS feet (v. 17).[1]

It seems to be increasingly apparent that there are a *variety of occasions* when, in the presence of a mighty work of God or of the Son of God Himself, men are brought to the ground before Him. We are reminded that we are but dust and were it not for the sustenance of God's Spirit, to dust we would return. (Gen. 3:19,Heb. 1:3)

(iii) ANGELS

> "... an angel of the Lord descended from Heaven and came and rolled back the stone and sat upon it ... and

---

1   cf. Daniel 10:8-20.

from fear of him the guards trembled (were shaken) and BECAME AS DEAD". (Matt. 28:2-4)

That God used an angel for the task of rolling away the stone of the tomb where Christ had been laid is plain. Whether the angel had the power to flatten the guards or whether it was a direct work of God's Holy Spirit is not so clear.

However, we can say that whatever the power of angels, its source is God; and we are right, when receiving angelic ministry and assistance in answer to our prayers, to give all the praise and glory to the Lord, for angels are messengers of God sent to minister on our behalf (Heb.1:14).

(iv) THE APOSTLES AND OTHER MEN

There is a valuable lesson to be learned from the three accounts of the apostle Paul's conversion, especially the last account recorded in the Scripture:

"Thus I journeyed to Damascus with the authority and commission of the chief priests. At midday, O king, I saw on the way a light from heaven brighter than the sun, shining round me and those who journeyed with me. AND WHEN WE HAD ALL FALLEN TO THE GROUND, I heard a voice saying to me in the Hebrew language, 'Saul, Saul, why do you persecute me? It hurts you to kick against the goads' (Acts 26:12-14)".
(See also Acts 9:3-6, 22:6-8)

From the above account of Paul's meeting with Jesus Christ on the road to Damascus, we can see that **not only did Paul fall to the ground, but also ALL HIS COMPANIONS**.

This would seem to indicate that they were not acting from a decision of the will, rationally convicted in their conscious minds by the drama of a supernatural light, but rather that, stunned and bewildered, their physical strength to stand was over-ruled by the power of God and **they crumpled to the ground as one man.**

Compare this with John Wesley's experience when preaching the gospel:

"One before me dropped as dead, and presently a second, and a third".

Wesley's Journal, 22nd June, 1739.

"Some sunk down and there remained no strength in them ..."

Wesley's Journal, 15th June, 1739.

"... for no sooner had he (Whitefield) begun (in the application of his sermon) to invite all sinners to believe in Christ, that four persons SANK DOWN close to him, almost in the same moment".

Wesley's Journal, 7th July, 1739.[1]

(cf. Journal entries 17,26 April; 1,12 May; 16 June; 1,30 July - all 1739).

From the growing weight of evidence it now seems apparent that God's Spirit fell power upon men, **removing their ability to stand before Him. He brought them to the ground** to deal with them in many and various ways, casting out demons and healing them in the innermost parts of their being. There is a practice today in many churches of ministering the power of God to many people who come forward for prayer, and as soon as the enquirer has gently hit the floor, the minister moves on down the prayer line to the next person. Some people like going forward for this kind of ministry because it is indeed restful and peaceful being under God's "anaesthetic"[2] Because

---

1   For these incidents in context, see Book 1.
2   cf. Gen. 2:21, 1 Sam. 26:12.

of this attention by God, many people believe that it is a sign of God's favour (grace) and draw the conclusion (quite wrongly) that those who are so affected are on a different spiritual wave-length to those who do NOT fall to the ground under God's power.

Certainly it is God's grace, but no soundly converted child of God needs a sign like that to convince them of God's goodness towards them. Secondly, it does NOT mean that only "spiritual people", i.e. higher-grade Christians, go "under the power" but rather the opposite. *In the majority of cases* it means, to be perfectly frank, that one is a child of God with bondages which the Lord wishes to remove.

You have problems He wants to deal with!

For example, when we go to an earthly doctor for treatment, it is because we know that something is wrong with us and we want him to heal us and make us better. Likewise in the spiritual realm. When we go to the Lord, we (all) know we need His help and His healing in many and various ways. When an earthly doctor anaesthetises us for an operation, it is for the purposes of removing something ugly, or straightening something out etc. - and if he were to do it while we were conscious, we would suffer great pain and shock, and perhaps have to be forcibly restrained, like **amputees** experienced before anaesthetics were discovered. So when the Lord applies His **spiritual** anaesthetic to His children through a minister, it is not normally His will that the minister move quickly on down the line to anaesthetise the others, never to return. With the subject under the restraining and restful hand of God, **NOW is the time to exercise healing and SPIRITUAL surgery and cast out the unclean spirits** discerned by the minister, in Jesus' Name. If going under the power of God is a sign at all, it is insufficient to only say that it is a sign of God's favour. Rather it is a sign to the minister to USE DISCERNMENT AND GET ON WITH THE JOB - not simply sail smugly on down the prayer line, satisfied that he has done his part. The battle has only just begun!

Using a "catcher"

In our own meetings Verlie and I feel reluctant to minister the power of God in the usual way, which is to have people stand in front of the minister, with a "catcher", usually a deacon, standing behind them. The minister then touches the forehead of the person being ministered to in Jesus' Name, and they (usually) fall backwards into the safe hands of the catcher and are lowered to the ground, where they remain "under the power" until the effect of the Spirit lifts away.

Our method

This method is unnecessary in our Deliverance and Restoration meetings and involves too many people for far too long, so we encourage our folk to slip out of their seats and make themselves comfortable on the carpet as soon as they feel themselves becoming drowsy in the Spirit. Most people learn to know when the power of God is coming on them and can put themselves down on the carpet before they go completely "under". This has the advantage of (i) freeing the ministers for the really important ministry and (ii) avoids the temptation of making a show and a gimmick out of God's power and grace, and (iii) drawing attention (glory?) to the minister rather than the Lord.

However, this is just a suggestion. Each minister must answer to the Lord for himself or herself regarding their methods of ministry.

Summary

Under the power of God difficult deliverance can be obtained with the minimum of fuss, drama and discomfort to both the Christian receiving and the Christian giving ministry. Physical force is rendered less necessary (*Mark* 9:26), and prayers for healing can bring outstanding results - praise God. When the power of God is operating it is *TIME TO DO BATTLE* and the Lord expects His ministers to co-operate with and be used by

His Spirit. Whoever heard of an earthly doctor anaesthetising his patients on the operating table and then leaving them unattended and untouched without operating until they regained consciousness? **The power of God's anaesthetic is not a gimmick for display.** It is a tool, a weapon, a provision whereby the Lord can both operate in our lives and **operate within our bodies,** which are temples of the Holy Spirit. Thus the Power of God is usually evidence or a sign that our gracious Lord wants to DO something in a Christian and that they are ready for ministry. It does not mean that they are more spiritual, but simply that the Lord wishes to work on them and in them. In like manner, **the deepness of one's spiritual anaesthetic** is usually an indication to the minister of the deepness of the needs of the Christian.

(v) THE NEED FOR POWER

"For men will be ... lovers of pleasure rather than lovers of God, HOLDING THE FORM OF RELIGION BUT DENYING THE POWER of it. Avoid such people". *(2 Tim.* 3:2-5)

If ever there was a scripture to make traditional Christian leaders sit up and take notice it would be this short passage from Paul to Timothy. For years traditional leaders have been telling their people to stay away from the (Charismatic) Renewal Movement and stick with the past conservative **traditions** of the historic Churches. The Bible says exactly the opposite. **It says to avoid the formalists** who have no Godly power flowing through their ministries, and thereby implies:

(i)   Powerless formalists are controlled by religious spirits.

(ii) Christians should fellowship where God's power is flowing, This is evidence of the presence and anointing of God's Holy Spirit.

"Do not forbid him" (who does a powerful work in my Name), said Jesus. (*Mark* 9:39)

These verses are a warning to Christians of every historic tradition who hammer the Word of God out on their own theological anvils to suit their own prejudices.

There must be no denying the ministry of casting out demons accomplished in Jesus' Name. To forbid is to contradict Christ's Word!

Some people say it is wrong to seek (spiritual) power; that Christians should seek humility rather than power. The Bible indicates that **our weakness** and **God's power** go hand in hand (2 Cor. 12:9-10). They are not mutually exclusive but inclusive. It is not an "either ... or" situation but "both ... and". They are not contradictory but complementary, as is so often the case with spiritual things.

We close this section with a summary from the New Testament of the early church's use of **the Power of God** to deliver and to heal:

★ "as though by our own *POWER* ... we had made him walk?" (asks Peter) (Acts 3:12).

★ "By what *POWER* ... did you do this?" (question the Jewish rulers) (Acts 4:7).

★ "so that they even carried out the sick into the streets, and laid them on beds and pallets, that as Peter came by *AT LEAST HIS SHADOW* might fall on some of them. The people also gathered from the towns around Jerusalem, bringing the sick and those afflicted with unclean spirits, and they were ALL healed" (Acts 5:15-16)

"the Lord ... granting **signs and wonders** to happen by their hands" (Acts 14:3).

★ "And God did extraordinary, *POWERFUL* deeds by the hands of Paul, so **handkerchiefs or aprons** were carried away from his body to the sick, and diseases left them and the evil spirits came out of them" (Acts

19:11-12).

★ "to win obedience ... by word and deed, by the *POWER* of signs and wonders, by the *POWER* of the Holy Spirit ..." (Rom. 15:18-19a).

"... the weapons of our warfare ... have divine *POWER* to destroy strongholds" (2 Cor. 10:4).

★ "Does He who supplies the Spirit to you and works *POWERFUL* deeds among you do so by the works of the law or by hearing with faith?" (Gal. 3:5).

★ "God also bearing witness by signs and wonders and various *POWERFUL* deeds and by **gifts of the Holy Spirit ...**" (Heb. 2:4-6)

These are a few selected references which give some idea of the emphasis "POWER" had in the ministry of the New Testament. **Note the unusual application of power for healing by Peter's shadow and Paul's aprons.** Such methods today might be condemned as superstitious or bizarre, but Luke records them matter-of-factly, the context of both passages indicating successful ministry. In our first quotation above Peter answers the astonishment of the Jews in Solomon's porch, "Why do you wonder at this or why do you stare at us ...?" and gives God the glory for the miraculous healing, when preaching Jesus of Nazareth before the rulers. (Acts 3:12)

Jesus' ministry is able to be continued by the early church because **they have His anointing** (Luke 4:18-19 with 1 John 2:26:27) **and His power** (John 20:21-23, Acts 1:8, 1 John 4:4). In the passages shown above, Power comes from the Lord, God, the Holy Spirit, the Spirit: and is described as divine; for the purpose of winning obedience, and witnessing; by faith and the distributions (gifts) of the Holy Spirit; and through the hands of the apostles.

SUCH POWER! How pale we are by comparison. And yet the

scriptures indicate that **the latter rain (of the Holy Spirit)** shall be greater than the former, so we can look forward to dramatic increases in the power of God granted to those who faithfully minister in Jesus' Name in the days that lie ahead. To this end **the prayers of the early church** can be examined by us with great spiritual profit:

> "And now, Lord, look upon their threats, and grant to thy servants to **speak Thy Word with all boldness,** while Thou stretchest out Thy hand to heal, and signs and wonders are performed through the name of Thy holy servant Jesus".
>
> And when they had prayed, the place in which they were gathered together was shaken; and they were all filled with the Holy Spirit and **spoke the Word of God with boldness" (Acts 4:29- 31).**

What a magnificent prayer by the early church! It just flows with POWER! The petition in verse 29 is that they might speak with boldness and verse 31 indicates that, having being filled with the Holy Spirit, "they spoke the word of God with boldness" (probably as soon as they left the place where they had been gathered). Can the modern church experience dramatic answers to prayers such as this? Yes - when it **prays and believes and ministers and suffers** for the Name of Jesus the way the early church did.

EPILOGUE

God's power is the key to the salvation ministries of **evangelism, deliverance and healing**, or indeed any dynamic Christian ministry. The Pharisees could "run rings around" the common people in theological debate, but they had no answer to the power of God. The Pharisees' clash with the man born blind is a classical example:

> **"... one thing I know, that though I was blind, now I see"** (John 9:25).

The apostles also shared the same experience of conflict with the Pharisees (Acts 4:13-14) but all the clever debate in the world perishes on the rock of the acts of the Holy Spirit's POWER! (1 Cor. 1:18-2:16).

The gift of the power to heal or to deliver people from unclean spirits is an anointing or commissioning from above; you either have it or you don't. Some have greater anointing than others and it seems that greater anointing is given with the accumulation of faithful ministry and experience and a deeper crucifixion with Christ. As we step out in faith and exercise the authority given to every Christian through the Word of God, so God answers our trust and gives us His power to minister.

Authority comes from the Word of God (i.e. what God has said) and **Power to minister comes from the Holy Spirit;** so that a combination of the Word and the Spirit gives us the combination of authority and power[1] that is needed for successful warfare. The "secret" is to EXERCISE our authority by *faith* in order that the power can begin to flow.

It is NOT simply the Word spoken in Jesus' Name ALONE. It is the Word spoken in Jesus' Name with authority AND by one who is given the power and/or anointing of God who succeeds where others fail. How do you receive this power? The same way you receive anything from God. You ask and you believe and you step out in faith, believing you have received. You carry out the authority the Word of God has already given you. The Lord answers by giving you a measure of power and He encourages you and trains you - increasing the measure of His power upon you as you learn and eliminate errors, and as you learn to listen to His Spirit.

Then, perhaps, one day, by the grace of God, you will share in the experience of Wesley, Whitefield and the Apostles before them.

---

1   See "Christian Authority and Power".

5.9 SELF-DELIVERANCE.

Now and again we hear a testimony from a Christian praising the Lord for deliverance received in private, either sovereignly from the Lord, or through ministry to oneself i.e. auto-or self-deliverance.

Any deliverance is a cause for praising the Lord and there is no question that the Lord may deliver a sufferer completely independently of a third party i.e. independently of a deliverance minister. However it would be most unwise for a sufferer to plan to embark on a course of self-deliverance as a normal program while there are competent deliverance ministers available to whom one could turn for ministry.

Why do we say that? Well, the reasons are many, as follows:

(i) WRONG MOTIVES

Why do people seek to be delivered privately, by themselves? Is it because they are **shy?** Or perhaps **embarrassed** by their personal problems? Is it because they are **lazy** or perhaps **too proud** to have anyone else know of their problems? I remember one young man who could not submit himself to our ministry. He preferred to submit himself to another very busy minister whom he knew could not possibly exercise any individual oversight over him because he already had a very large congregation to pastor. So what do you do when you know you should be under the covering authority of a pastor, yet you hate submitting to such authority? You simply "submit" yourself to a very busy man and lose or hide yourself in his hundreds of sheep. This way you can deceive yourself, and others, by giving the appearance of submitting to authority without actually having any effective oversight laid on you. Therefore **self-deliverance could also be expression of rebellion against the ministry authority of a third party.** All these motives are unworthy of a sincere Christian.

(ii) LACK OF DISCERNMENT.

When we minister to ourselves it can be difficult for us to obtain **clear, unclouded discernment. Deliverance ministry stirs up the mind and soul** of the sufferer so that things can become confused for a season. Such confusion of mind can hinder the operation of the gift of discerning of spirits, which operation is vital for effective ministry. People who practise self-deliverance are **simply not clear-sighted enough** to know what is going on, while an independent third party who is ministering does not suffer this disadvantage. At the very best, the judgement or discernment of a person who is undergoing deliverance could only be described as limited.

(iii) LACK OF DISCIPLINE

My youngest son Kip is a very good swimmer and recently when we were on holidays over Christmas-New Year, he was given a program by his swimming coach to maintain while he was away with us. He was not only given a full program but also minimum levels to maintain. He enjoys swimming and fully intended to maintain the top program but-you've guessed it-when it came down to actually performing on the day, he settled for the minimum because there was no coach watching over him. His reason? He was on holidays, didn't feel like it, too much else to do, I'll do better tomorrow etc. etc.

I think that these excuses sound familiar to most of us because WE have used them at some time or another.

People who practise self–deliverance need a great deal of self–discipline. Some Christians have it, but most of us do not, and ministry sessions become few and far between. When arrangements are made to meet with a deliverance minister, things are just that much harder to wriggle out of. The Lord knows that the opposition within the sufferer's soul just prior to a deliverance session can be very heavy indeed. How much easier it is to defect when we only have to send our apologies for not attending a deliverance session today TO

OURSELVES!

(iv) LACK OF HONESTY

If we minister to ourselves we are placed in the position of having to **pick and choose what spirits we want to get rid of.** We may even say, "The Lord told me ..." in order to convince ourselves we are on the right track, but my experience has been that those who follow this course are far too gentle with themselves. They use what **Bob Mumford** once described as a **"rubber hammer"** on themselves, making sure that they don't hurt too much. We are not honest enough or severe enough on ourselves for the obvious reason that we are both minister and patient at the one time and cannot afford to lose control of the situation. Mental and spiritual control must be kept at all times by the minister (ourselves?) and this means that manifestations must be kept low key and easily manageable, which, of course, limits the ministry enormously.

We once ministered to a professional rock musician who needed consistent ministry. All was proceeding quite encouragingly until we began to nominate and command the **spirit of musical hypnosis** to come out which, of course, put the finger of God upon his consuming passion, and perhaps even his livelihood, and he quickly ceased coming for ministry. Had he ministered to himself he would never have commanded that spirit out of himself, yet his interest in **heavy rock music, which is really witchcraft music,** was the basis of all his mind-control problems. I suggest that most of us have touchy areas deep down with which we don't really want the Lord to interfere. The bottom line is that we can LIKE some of our unclean-ness and DON'T ALWAYS WANT TO CHANGE some areas in ourselves.

(v) NEED OF SUPPORT

Going through deliverance ministry, especially deep-seated soulish deliverance, is not an easy experience. Our total personality is put under the scrutiny of God's Holy Spirit, who begins to search us out in our inward parts. Does not the Word of God say:

> "The heart is more deceitful than all else and is desperately sick (wicked). Who can understand it? I, the Lord, search the heart..." (Jer. 17:9 – 10a)

When this is happening, we need support; **support from our brothers and sisters in Christ - people we know and trust,** and who themselves know something of what is happening to us. We need people who can **support us in prayer and fellowship with us.** Speaking for myself now, I would regard self or private deliverance as putting myself under unnecessary pressure and stress. When I was receiving ministry I needed someone else to minister the Lord Jesus to me, and I believe that anyone who tries self-deliverance when there are other trustworthy deliverance ministers available, is making things unnecessarily difficult for themselves.

In conclusion, there are many advantages in receiving deliverance ministry from a third party, someone who will **monitor the ministry** we are receiving from the Lord, week by week, and day by day; someone who will **help us to help ourselves**, who will **give unclouded discernment;** who will **not be influenced by unclean motives** or **lack of honesty** (because we do not know what is in our heart); and last, but not least, someone who can **minister the presence of the Lord Jesus to us** when the battle is hardest.

If we receive deliverance ministry on Sundays, there will probably be many occasions during the week when we will receive further ministry, in private, but that is not really self-deliverance but a flow-on from the regular Sunday ministry which is monitoring the whole week.

So then, when we have a choice, let us choose to submit ourselves to a faithful ministry and let the Lord have His way, without reservations. Hallelujah!

5.10 DISTANT AND PROXY MINISTRY.

(i) MINISTRY FROM A DISTANCE.

One of the more astonishing things about the ministry of the Lord Jesus when He walked the earth was **His authority over time and space,** in the sense that He healed and delivered people with whom He had no physical contact at all because they lay sick in another part of the country.

Both the healing of the centurion's servant (Matt.8:5-13) and the deliverance of the syro-phoenician woman's daughter (Mark 7:25- 30) have so much to teach us, but perhaps the main point of each story is that Jesus healed and delivered them AT A DISTANCE and the need to lay on hands, or even be physically present was unnecessary.

We practice this **ministry at a distance** today, ministering continuous deliverance and healing to Christians in Queensland, Newcastle and Canberra (in Australia), U.S.A., South Africa, Philippines and England, and the necessary arrangements and conditions for ministry are set out in our application form (See Appendix G). We are pleased to say that the results have been very encouraging in the majority of cases, but as would be expected, **more Christian discipline is required** from the sufferer so that they "tune in" spiritually to the ministry in Sydney at the right time of day, thus joining in with us in spirit without the advantage of being surrounded by our fellowship physically.

(ii) PROXY MINISTRY

This is so-called when someone "stands in" for healing or deliverance on behalf of someone else who is in need of ministry, but who cannot be present in the flesh. It has been exercised quite successfully by various healing ministers but there doesn't appear to be much of this practice in deliverance work. Perhaps the reason is that there are many more "healers" than there are "deliverers". And yet it ought not to be so. It is true that Jesus **HEALED the centurion's servant** with a word from a distance in response to the centurion's plea for help, and it is just as true that Jesus **DELIVERED the Syro-phoenician woman's daughter** from a severe demon - also with a word from a distance in response to a plea for help. In each case the pleader had a **close relationship** with the sufferer and **exercised a strong saving faith** (of a quality that put Jewish believers to shame) **on behalf of the sufferer,** and it is these BASIC PRINCIPLES upon which the proxy ministry operates.

Maybe the Christian church doesn't have too many people around who can speak a word and get results like Jesus, unhindered by time and geographical space; but if we have legitimate proxies to stand in for loved ones in need, then there is no reason why we cannot minister to the stand-in (who would obviously be exercising faith and compassion) on behalf of the absent sufferer.

A counsellor's son

One lady counsellor was concerned about her schoolboy son who was going through a destructive and rebellious phase of his growing–up. The lady counsellor was getting nowhere using the normal methods that a mother uses to obtain obedience from growing boys and in desperation requested that she go proxy in deliverance ministry for her lad.

When the ministry began she manifested powerfully (just as if *she* was receiving ministry) and there can be no question amongst those present (including myself) that her boy was receiving strong ministry. When she went home that night, her son met her with popping eyes - "Mum, I don't know what's happened to me but I'm as weak as water - I can't raise my arms there is no strength in them or in my legs - I can hardly lift a finger - what's wrong with me?" Smilingly his mother brushed away his fears and reassured him, while giving silent praise to God. She knew full well that evil, destructive strength had been removed from him and he would recover soon enough.

Ministry to "fringe" people

Proxy ministry presents to Christians who are prepared to step into the breach themselves, an opportunity to obtain successful ministry for loved ones who may be recalcitrant, rebellious, apathetic, unbelieving, perverse, or simply unavailable - and perhaps set them on the road to full salvation in Jesus Christ our Lord. I would have to say that there is **no record of the exact equivalent** of this form of ministry in the New Testament, but it works. If it is compassionate and is performed to the glory of Jesus it simply embodies the principles of Jesus' ministry to subjects over a distance. **However it should only be used as a last resort.**

I believe this form of ministry also embodies the principle that **"the unbelieving husband/man is sanctified by the believing wife/woman, and the unbelieving wife/woman is sanctified by the believing husband/man; otherwise your children would be unclean, but now they are holy."** (1 Cor. 7:4). Even though this is given to us in the context of a man and woman and their children where only one parent is a Christian, Paul distinctly conveys the principle that **the unbeliever is sanctified by the believer, and that our children are also sanctified by the believing parent.** The conclusion is surely that *the Christian believer has enormous influence and authority for the Kingdom of God within his or her family.* To sanctify means to (make) holy, to separate for God's use and purpose; thus proxy ministry by a Christian for members of his or her immediate family (except perhaps children for adults) seems to be valid, even for unbelievers - one might say *especially for unbelievers!* **The very causes of the unbelief can be removed by the faith of the believer!** What is the basis for the authority we are grasping from this word? Is it the headship of a man over his family (and himself under the headship of Christ)? Yes, that has relevance, but even more than that, because you will notice that while the believing man sanctifies his wife and his children, it is also true that **the believing woman sanctifies her unbelieving husband, aside from his headship over her.** What then is the basis of this authority of the woman? It is not headship, but **the one-flesh relationship.** But, you say she is not one-flesh with her children! But are they not of her own flesh and blood and a product of the one-flesh relationship? Let me try to explain this one-flesh principle.

When a man and woman marry they become one flesh, according to the scriptures. They are two distinct persons, but the glory of sexual intercourse at its highest and most meaningful level (apart from being an expression of deep intimacy and affection, and effecting procreation) is that it fuses two bodies together and makes them one flesh in the sight of God. Paul puts it this way:

> "... husbands aught also to love their own wives as their own bodies. **He that loves his own wife loves himself;** for no man ever hates his own flesh, but nourishes it and cherishes it, even as Christ also the church, because we are members of His body. For this cause shall a man leave his father and mother, and shall cleave to his wife; and the two shall become one flesh" (Eph. 5:28-31).

Therefore when one married person becomes a dwelling place or temple of the Holy Spirit, that situation not only changes the spouse that has been so blessed but **it affects the other spouse–the other half of the one-flesh unity. When one is blessed, he or she becomes a channel or an agency for blessing the other.** Hence the unbelieving spouse is sanctified by the believing - and the blessing flows on down to their own flesh and blood - the children.

Problems after a conversion

Is it any wonder that spouses react strongly when one half of the one-flesh union is converted? Usually there is either a double conversion fairly quickly OR great resistance from the agencies of satan within the unbelieving spouse. I believe there would be a lot more double conversions if the believing spouse:

(i)   could diagnose the root cause of their opposition, AND
(ii)   knew how to use the spiritual weapons available, and
(iii)   did so.

Proxy ministry is one of these latter weapons, for the unbelieving spouse is sanctified by the believing, and so are the children.

Do you have a loved one for whom you have been praying for what seems like 100 years, and with no effectual response? Perhaps they are being prevented from responding by power of doubt, unbelief, fear or confusion etc? Well, God has provided a way for them - through you - because they are sanctified by *your* faith - and those spiritual blocks can be removed-through you, if you are prepared to stand in for them. **It is not light decision** to make but you can ask the Lord for guidance in this matter, and also talk with your Pastor and/or Deliverance minister regarding whether you are in a sufficiently strong spiritual relationship with the Lord yourself to take on someone else's burden of deliverance as well as your own. It is not easy.

(iii) TWO WORDS OF WARNING

(a)   PROXY MINISTRY IS NOT A MAGIC FORMULA. It seems to be successful in removing spiritual blocks which have prevented the exercise of faith in Jesus Christ as Saviour and Lord. It has the effect of freeing up the human will from the reign of unclean spirits so that an unbeliever CAN make the right choice. **However if this freedom is NOT used** and the unbeliever CHOOSES to stay in rebellion by a decision of the human will and spirit, then one of two things may happen. Either:

(a)   the unbeliever will be the subject of severe corrective action permitted by the Lord (Rom.

11:22), or;

(b) worst of all, God withdraws and leaves them to their choice of death (Rom. 1:24,26,28).

The point is, what have you (if you are the believing spouse) or they, got to lose? I believe the unbelieving spouse must be given every opportunity through whatever weapons of ministry the Lord has provided. If we do all we can in Christ Jesus, then we will save many souls; and those we lose will not be laid to our charge.

(b) PROXY MINISTRY IS NOT EASY for the person standing-in for the sufferer. As they submit to ministry they will not only be going into battle for the sufferer but they will be receiving ministry for themselves also. That is to say, they receive ministry for TWO people, when some people struggle to battle through just for themselves.

Our normal practice is not to accept applications for proxy until a person has received substantial ministry for themselves and is coping well. However it goes without saying that the Holy Spirit's leading must be followed, and normally this leading will be given to the deliverance minister. If in doubt one can always allow the volunteer stand-in to begin, and then monitor their progress regularly. If ministry becomes too heavy for them, cease the double ministry immediately.

They can always try again later.

If you believe the Lord is happy about you going proxy, and your deliverance minister witnesses to this, then do not be afraid, for your miracle-working God will break the grip of the enemy upon your household and at least give your spouse a chance to respond to Christ.

Praise the Name of the Lord!

(iv) IMPORTANT NOTE

It is possible to combine Distant ministry AND Proxy ministry. Praise the Lord again!

5. 11 COMPLETING A SESSION

Deliverance sessions, whether single or group, can be very exhausting or very exhilarating, or can leave you with a quiet sense of praising God–and sometimes a mixture of all three. You never quite know what condition you are going to be in at the finish of a session. There are exhausting times both physically and spiritually, but the blessing of the sessions more than makes up for them. For normal deliverance groups you would use team work wherever possible, of course, and it seems to be the general case that you won't be able to get everything unclean out that you aimed at in one session. I cannot remember a case, a single case, where we have actually finished all **attempted** deliverance to the satisfaction of all within an hour. I know Jesus did; I am quite sure the Apostles did; and perhaps, one day, so will we - but **at the present time it is necessary to exercise continuous ministry,** whether for PARTICULAR or TOTAL[1] cleansing, because one session of an hour and a half is quite long enough for one-to-one ministry, both from the minister's point of view and the subject's point of view. It may not be sufficient to completely free a Christian of a particular problem and so we may have to bind or tie things over until another session. We do that in the context of prayer and in four basic ways.

Wind down (normalising)

Firstly, we switch off any tape-recorded ministry that may be playing in support of those ministering, and vocal ministry is ceased. Unclean spirits that are still on the way out are

---

1   See "End-Time Deliverance" for a full discussion.

commanded to leave quickly, but all others are to settle down and await further instructions. It sounds incredible to order unclean spirits to stop manifesting and leaving but you have to draw the line somewhere if you are going to close off a session and leave the subject in a reasonably clear state of mind with which to go out onto the street. After a few minutes things will be reasonably quiet. There may be the odd subject who needs help in removing a spirit that is nearly out but appears stuck (sometimes in the throat). A few sharp commands in the ear is usually sufficient to shift the culprit but you must either get rid of it (preferably) or make it settle back before they leave the meeting. It is not good to leave it in the throat area as experience shows it can be quite discomforting and may leave the subject later in public and perhaps embarrassing circumstances. If there is any doubt the sufferer should stay awhile after the meeting and enjoy some informal fellowship, just to make sure they go home in good shape.

Binding orders

Assuming that ministry has ceased satisfactorily and the manifestations are settling down as commanded, the **second step** is to **bind** all unclean spirits from manifesting any further during the coming days and nights. They are commanded to be SILENT, INACTIVE and HARMLESS by night and by day. The sufferers are to be allowed to sleep the sleep of the beloved in Christ (Psalm 127:2) without anxiety or nightmares. They are not to be troubled at their work or at play, or in their domestic situations. **The powers of darkness are thus totally straight-jacketed** in the Name of the Father, and of the Son, and of the Holy Spirit, which name is the Name of the Lord Jesus;[1] and they are told they MUST obey these commands, with two exceptions permitted:

> (i)   They may go to their appointed place (laid down at the beginning of the session) AT ANY TIME,

---

[1]   The singular Name of the baptismal formula (Matt. 28:19) used throughout the Acts of the Apostles.

provided they do not manifest in any way that hurts, discomforts, embarrasses or distresses the sufferer.

(ii) They MUST go DURING ANY CHRISTIAN FELLOWSHIP or ACTIVITY such as praise, reading the Word, prayer, listening to sermons etc.

— quickly and quietly!

— otherwise they are to remain totally inactive until the next ministry session.

These orders apply by night as well as by day; otherwise some folk are going to lose sleep and that inevitably means that you will too. Quite apart from compassionate reasons we have a very sound self-interest in the welfare of our sufferers at night-time! There are more than enough night disturbances for the Christian shepherd to contend with and a **sound authoritative binding** on the demons will certainly reduce problems for both subject and minister.

However, these directions can be adjusted as the minister is led by the Holy Spirit. There may be times when it may not be wise to command or invite continuous ministry during the forthcoming week for certain cases due to possible drama that could eventuate. At other times you may be led to command continuous removal during waking hours; but with most groups we have found that *permission to go at any time and the command to go during any Christian activity* (always under the conditions laid down - silently and harmlessly) are best.

The method we have outlined here as fairly normal (that of commanding demons to go during Christian activities, and permitting them to go at any time providing they obey the standing orders to be silent and harmless) has the effect of *PROVIDING MINISTRY ON A SEVEN-DAYS-A-WEEK BASIS,* as the Holy Spirit dictates.

This means that your weekly ministry meeting (on Sundays?) acts as a *monitoring cover* over what is going on. Thus you normally see the sufferers at least once a week in order to

> (i)   check on their progress personally,
> (ii)   receive discernment on their behalf and
> (iii) minister to the situation you see them in;
> (iv) give them some solid relevant teaching and encouragement, and
> (v)   keep them praising and worshipping the Lord.

But, of course, the ministry continues for the rest of the week. It does not stop altogether because although they are out of *YOUR* sight, they are not out of the *LORD'S* sight! They continue to receive ministry from Him actively according to their needs and their involvement with the Lord, and the Sunday deliverance meeting becomes a valuable check-point as well as an opportunity to meet with the Great Deliverer.

Thirdly, we pray and ask the Lord to fill everyone with His Holy Spirit. The New Testament commands us to **be filled with the Spirit (Eph. 5:18). It is an imperative command of the Word of God. It commands us to be on fire with the Spirit** (Rom. 12:11) and the Lord Jesus Christ has taught us to ask and we shall receive (Luke 11:13). So we ask for that which He has commanded, and we say, **"In the Name of Jesus Christ, be filled with the Spirit"** to a subject. By that we don't necessarily mean totally filled, but everything which is available, clean, washed out, ready, waiting for the Lord to take over - *every department,* if I can use a physical word, *which has been emptied out, we give to the Lord to fill with Himself.* I believe we can increase in the measure of the Holy Spirit more and more as we are set free from the occupancy of the forces of darkness. More recently I have been praying for the Lord to fill EVERY area of His temples, polluted and clean.

Fourthly, the subject is committed into the Lord's hands for protection, guidance and blessing until the next session. It is one thing to get a fellow in the church building and to pray with him and see buckets of alcoholic spirits moved out, but it is another thing to have to send him back out into the streets amongst his "friends," who will quickly draw him back into their fold. For so many it is back into the gutter to share the common bottle which is the symbol of a fellowship of slavery. *At the very least,* we need so much to commit those who have received ministry into the Lord's hands for His protection and guidance until we see them in order to minister Jesus to their souls again.

At this point it may be necessary to command those who are under the power of God to open their eyes and "Wake up in Jesus' Name!" Once the ministry of deliverance has been completed, the ministry of the power of God has served its purpose and it is wise to get the people fully mobile as quickly as the Lord will permit. **Beware of actors** and **people seeking special attention** and **extra ministry unnecessarily**. Selfishness on the part of people here can easily result in the minister becoming overtired to the point of spiritual exhaustion, which serves satan's purposes, not God's.

Genuine cases of manifesting, of course, should be attended to before the sufferer goes home. Either the troublesome spirits must be bound up effectively, or removed, and the remainder bound up to be silent, inactive and harmless. The minister has to learn to be able to distinguish between genuine cases and those that are simply attention-seeking. In any event, a demon that is just surfacing in the personality will not last or stay very long. Our normal practice is to have some fellowship over light refreshments after the ministry, and as most people stay on for this happy time in the flush of the Lord's blessing and liberty, it provides the opportunity for observing those who are caught in some brief difficulty. Many a time we have needed to reassure someone manifesting awkwardly at the close of a meeting by telling them not to worry – it is on its way out and will be gone in a few moments. We always **carefully double-check** such cases before they go home.

In the final analysis you are as close and as available to your people as the telephone, and also you will see many of them again at the meeting next week at the very latest, God willing.

5.12 DON'TS

Some cautions are worth considering for individual or small controlled-group deliverance situations. For example, you will remember that it is important that **the minds and spirits of the subjects be focussed on the Lord Jesus Christ and kept there** throughout the session. By far the easiest and most spiritually enjoyable way of doing this is to worship the Lord with music and song. Also **obedience to the instructions of the deliverance ministers and counsellors** is very important. During the ministry this should be an unquestioned obedience similar to that required of any soldier of an army engaging an enemy. Unity of spirit and purpose is vital, and questions can be answered later, when the heat of the battle is over. Satan will attempt to divert and distract every mind, and by means of the mind, every human spirit, but this must be resisted. Once they have entered "into the spirit" through praise and worship, they must stay "in the spirit" and not be distracted by the things of the flesh.

Likewise deliverance counsellors should keep "in the spirit" and not be distracted by personalities and emotional involvement with people they know and love. I would roughly liken it to nurses in a large general hospital who exercise caring attention but who know their patients more by their infirmities than their names. They know Mrs. Bloggs as "the appendectomy" and Mr. Brown as "the tonsillectomy" at the end of the ward. It sounds impersonal but in fact it means that the counsellors are concentrating on the real problem in the spiritual realm, and not allowing themselves to be distracted. *That* is true Christian love in action. The Holy Spirit is no respecter of persons and the counsellors are there to minister according to *His* leading without regard to fleshly or soulish considerations. The COMPASSION OF CHRIST will equip you all to attack the PROBLEM but beware the deceit of the sympathy of the

FLESH which can be a satanic ploy to "draw the teeth" of your ministry and thus render you ineffective (e.g. by feeding the self-pity or mourning and grieving in your sufferer).

Prayer Style

It is generally better for counsellors to **use authoritative commands** given in the Name of Jesus rather than healing prayer, although there is certainly room for the latter during ministry. Remember that deliverance is authoritative and healing will flow from spiritual surgery.

No talk

Counsellors should not engage in **protracted conversation** with subjects (or with unclean spirits) because this can be done later. The people are there for MINISTRY and it is not possible for the mind and the spirit to be focussed on Jesus during lengthy chatter. **Keep talk by subjects to the necessary minimum.**

No physical abuse

It is very important that male counsellors act properly in the ministry to lady sufferers. Where the laying on of hands is desirable this should be done in a manner which can cause no offence whatsoever. It is up to the minister in charge to ensure that Christ's Name is not brought into disrepute by an unclean intrusion into His ministry.

All these basic "ground" rules are rules which have been tested in spiritual warfare and which have been found to work for the benefit of all because I believe they were inspired by the Holy Spirit. We gain the impression from the New Testament that Jesus and the apostles practised widespread deliverance but we are given few practical details regarding methods; so I am not saying that every Christian leader should minister the same way that we do, but I am saying that such guidelines were good for us and we share them with you for your consideration and use where appropriate.

Let us summarise some of the cautions advised so far and add a few more that are worth recording as follows:

(i) PREPARATION

1) **DON'T attempt ministering alone without obtaining experience** in assisting other deliverance ministers in action. Having said that as a general guideline of great importance, it is obvious to all of us that there will be exceptions. It is distinctly possible that you will be forced into doing something that you have never done before, and the Lord may put you into a situation where you are called upon to minister and that's all there is about it. But I am saying that you ought to first assist other counsellors for the purpose of gaining experience, if possible. Let your deliverance minister and/or pastor know that you would like to assist them in this work.

2) **DON'T jump into one-on-one ministry without adequate prior counselling** with the subject, whenever this is possible. During counselling the subject should reveal their activities,[1] occult or immoral, or something like that. They should reveal their character weaknesses, such as fear, or rages, or deceit, or experiences such as nightmares, which gives the "growing" minister a very good lead in where to start. Other problems will come to light as progress is made. Even the Lord Jesus who had gifts of wisdom, knowledge, and discerning of spirits etc. practised counselling as necessary.

Again, this caution is for single ministry by appointment. However, as was the case with the apostles, there may be times nominated by the Holy Spirit when you will spiritually take the enemy by the scruff of the neck and throw him out from a perfect stranger. Just be sure the Lord is overruling in such situations!

---

1   See Book 1, Chapter 4,2.

3) **DON'T deliberately minister deliverance to anyone who has not made a commitment to Jesus Christ as Lord** of their life. Remember that if the Holy Spirit does not move in to replace the cast-out demons, the last state of the person could well be seven times worse than before the ministry. So remember that, please - it is most important. I know that in Gospel days Jesus ministered and, in the timing of God, the Holy Spirit had not yet been poured out; but now the Spirit of God is available to us all and **He must be asked and prayed in to replace every foul and unclean thing** that has gone, that we may grow in the fulness of the Holy Spirit. Again, there must be exceptions such as evangelistic situations, or a clash with a disruptive spirit in an occultist (Acts 16:16f), or large meetings. Just be sure you are led by the Holy Spirit when departing from this guideline.

4) **DON'T forget your divine weapons** for the pulling down of strongholds. (2 Cor. 10:3-6) - we discussed a number of them under the heading "Preparation of the Minister" - (Chapter 3, Book1).

(ii) AUTHORITY AND TEAMWORK

5) **DON'T forget to give all the praise and the glory to the Lord Jesus at regular intervals** during your victories (the remaining demons will hate this, too), i.e. don't lose your joy in the Lord. Some people wonder why Christian "exorcists" look so cheerful. A quick reference to the Christian disciples' early experiences (Luke 10:17-20) will inform us of two very good reasons indeed, but beware of pride. (Isa. 14:12-20)

Down through the years I have seen many sincere Christians enter into deliverance work and some of them have "burned out" within two years, because of the huge demands made on their time and spiritual "reserves". I have said in another place that Deliverance Ministers need to have their basic Christian disciplines of prayer, Bible study, praise and fellowship well and truly established in their Christian walk if they are going to maintain effective ministry over the long term.

If we can hold our disciplines in place, which is another way of saying if we can draw close and KEEP close to our Heavenly Father and His only begotten Son then we will never lose our JOY, and the joy of the Lord really is our daily source of strength (Neh. 8:10).

6) **DON'T forget to work under pastoral authority wherever possible.** Endeavour to obtain your minister's oversight. Try to engage the co-operation of spiritually-sensitive medical consultants with difficult subjects, although I regret to say, at the time of writing, that may be very difficult-even impossible. Unfortunately, **scientific training appears to build enormous intellectual barriers against seeing physical sickness in spiritual terms,** even though the two are plainly mutually inclusive, not exclusive. The advantages of keeping violent patients sedated in-between deliverance sessions, and safe in trained hands that are spiritually aware must surely be obvious.

7) **DON'T encourage self-deliverance,** except under pastoral eyes and authority. The advantages of another person monitoring the sufferer's progress with unclouded discernment, honesty and compassion, and supplying plenty of back-up prayer support and encouragement when we need it, must be obvious to all. (see chapter 5, section 9).

8) **DON'T endeavour to minister deliverance ALONE** if at all possible, even when experienced. Always try to have a chaplain or assistant with you in order to **witness the truth** and to **add faith, power, voice** and **prayer support.** In any case, you ought to be training up-and-coming deliverance ministers whenever possible and many young people would be "blessed out of their socks" to assist an experienced man or woman in, spiritual warfare. Compare the privilege of David as Saul's armour-bearer (1 Sam 16:21)

9) **DON'T minister deliverance quickly to anyone dangerous who is not prepared to give you written permission** to do so. It may be that you do not actually want permission in writing but simply want to sort out the sincerity of

the "dangerous" person. If they don't want to give you written permission it may well be they are a satanic agency sent to bring your ministry down by self – destructing after you have begun ministering to them. If the person is not mentally or physically capable of doing so, permission should be obtained from next of kin. (See Book 1 -Appendix "C")

These comments obviously apply to a situation where counselling is possible before ministry. Should the Lord throw you suddenly into a deliverance battle you can be sure you will be given the power to win and get Him glory.

So make SURE you do! – Before you send them home.

10) **DON'T lose control of the ministry,** over both those who receive and those who assist you (in the Lord) in ministering, i.e. your ministering team. You cannot afford to have patients dictating the terms of your ministry to them, i.e. how they want to be ministered to - how, where, when and for what. If the patient is going to be in control and dominate the minister - even in attitude rather than practice - then there is **no submission and no trust, and the Holy Spirit will not be able to lead you.** The whole ministry will become an exercise in futility and uncleanness. YOU make clear the terms – according to the Word of God and the leading of His Spirit.

Likewise, it is important for your co-workers to keep one eye and ear open for your instruction during groups. In the early stages you may not think this is necessary, but as your discernment grows it will be very necessary. **Watch out for any unclean manifestation in your co-workers as well as the patients.** Generally speaking, males should lay hands on males, and females on females, to avoid heterosexual activity (except, of course, in the case of homosexuals). If the patients are prone on the floor under the power of God, make sure they are "handled" carefully and sensitively. **Counsellors should never use their feet,** or allow their contempt of the unclean spirits to manifest itself disrespectfully towards the patients lying on the floor - that conduct would itself spring from an unclean source. If there is anything unclean in a counsellor, it will usually emerge and manifest during the ministry after a few meetings and it is not unusual for counsellors to become patients. If they are too proud to receive ministry for themselves, they should not be counselling anyway.

11) **DON'T let sufferers depart after ministry until binding commands** (see previous section) **have been given,** and the fulness of the Holy Spirit prayed in for each sufferer. If somebody wants to rush away, they should wait for the appropriate "closing" of the ministry before departing, or alternatively you can appoint a counsellor to "bind them up" straightaway, and let them go before the end. If the unclean spirits misbehave and take the sufferer out of the doors before there is time to "close off," then binding etc. of the sufferer must be done immediately (in the sufferer's physical absence), preferably with support of the faith of other helpers, in order to prevent the sufferer harming himself or herself, or anyone else.

12) **DON'T tell anyone they are completely healed or completely delivered,** i.e. never put words into anyone's mouth. Let them bear testimony to what the Lord has done for them. Well-meaning but inaccurate and false testimonies in the past have harmed the cause of Christ. This is not to say that we should not acknowledge and confess what the Word of God says in our times of fellowship with the Lord and other Christians, but *our testimony to others must be TRUE in the material realm,* not only in the spiritual realm.

Presumption and exaggeration are sins. (Num. 15:30, Psa. 19:13).

Sometimes in deliverance work a minister will pray briefly and tell the sufferer they are free, but unfortunately it is not true, either in the spiritual or the physical. The spirit is just lying silent for the moment and laughing quietly to itself until it's safe to emerge and manifest itself again.

13) **DON'T mistake wishful thinking for faith,** and remember

that faith (trust! - not easy believism) is the basis for all victory in spiritual warfare but not necessarily INSTANT victory. The measure of the Power of God flowing through the ministry is also an essential factor.

14) **DON'T get over-confident** with early or dramatic successes (Luke 10:17) which the Lord gives you to encourage and train you, because the day will surely come, and soon, when you will fail (Mark 9:18,28).

Not God, not the sufferer, but YOU will fail for one reason or another (examined in Book 3, Chapter 9). **You will learn more from ONE failure than TEN victories,** and most of what you learn will be about yourself. NO-one becomes a complete OVERCOMER OVERNIGHT!

When you go into battle, give it all you've got, with joy, in the Name of the Lord. Over-confidence (pride) because of previous easy victories etc. will rob you of your battle-tuning and preparedness, and blunt your sensitivity to the leading of the Holy Spirit. **Never become independent of Him but learn to become totally dependent.** The more anointed you are the more dependent you should be (and vice versa).

For me, that continues to be a daily lesson which is easier said than done.

CHAPTER 6

AFTER THE BEGINNING

The deliverance subjects under your care will need to know that they are being shepherded by a true shepherd of Christ in that **any attempt to deceive or distress them after the actual ministry should be put down immediately.** We may not always think so, but the telephone is a wonderful invention and it is advisable to give them at least certain times of the day when you know you will be in your study, or not far away. **Now that the orders to leave have been given, batches of demons might leave at any time of the day or night,** so the subjects need to be warned to notice anything unusual - such as periods of coughing, hiccoughing, yawning, sneezing, aches and pains, or frequent visits to the toilet. Occasionally a person will experience the whole gamut of unclean emotions - bitterness, loneliness, etc. etc. - but this is not bad, but good, because the spirits are simply manifesting themselves prior to or during release. The subject simply **hangs on to Jesus through praise etc. and release will come.** It is easier said than done, but it **must be done,** and in any case, *there is no other advice* for the Christian sufferer. Symptoms are GOOD news, not bad. They are a cause for PRAISE, not alarm, in the vast majority of deliverance situations.

1. THE NEED FOR CONTINUOUS MINISTRY

We need to say some more about the need for continuous ministry in relation to ongoing problems (see chapter 5.1 (ii) (c)).

Continuing problems

At the very beginning, I made the mistake of thinking that one ministry session - even one spirit cast out - and the job was done. I sent the person away believing them to be cleansed and expecting no more trouble. But when the sufferer came back three months later, still in trouble, I did not make the mistake (still prevalent today) of thinking that they had not held their deliverance, either due to unbelief or bad life-style and habits, and that the spirit had returned to them. This sort of failure can happen, of course, and MAY be the reason for continuing problems; but, in my experience, the vast majority of continuing problems indicate, not failure by the subject, but simply that the ministry has only removed the tip of the iceberg. An iceberg manifests approximately one-ninth of its substance above the ocean where it can be seen, while eight-ninths remains submerged. However, if we were to remove the visible one-ninth from the top, that would not mean that the iceberg would become invisible, with its whole mass below the surface. No - the iceberg would adjust itself so that even thought it was smaller now, one-ninth would appear above and eight-ninths below the waves.

The laws of nature are such that **we only ever see one-ninth of the total danger manifesting itself.** The proportions may be different but **sin is like that, and unclean spirits are like that - and the answer is regular ministry.** This subject is the matter of other books[1] in which the nature of sin, unclean spirits, the flesh, the old man, the man of sin etc. and their relationship to each other are discussed; but for now it is important to accept the principle that spasmodic, once-every-five-years deliverance is not even scratching the surface of the iceberg of problems in many Christians, and that if you want your Church members to experience GENUINE freedom of their (human) spirits and GENUINE fulness of the Holy Spirit - then **regular ministry should be made available** to them, as required.

Some will argue that the Lord Jesus never needed to minister regularly to sufferers in the New Testament but there are several factors to be considered when we compare the ministry today with Jesus' visit in the flesh to the world. We would need to consider:

---

1   e.g. "Your Full Salvation" and Book 4 "Discerning Human Nature."

1) Jesus' primary and secondary missions during His earthly walk. **His primary mission was obviously to become the sacrificial Lamb of God** who took away the sin of the world. Preaching the Kingdom of God, fulfilling the Law of Moses, establishing a New Covenant and revealing God the Father in His own person are other vital accomplishments. The working of healing, deliverance and other miracles are secondary to the main mission. They demonstrate the divinity of Jesus as the Son of God, the goodness and compassion of God and the reality of His Kingdom, and were not intended to do much more than that.

2) **The comparative spiritual cleanliness of law-abiding Israel** to whom Jesus ministered compared to the abominable practices of the Gentiles and their (Canaanitish) Gentile, occult, demonic cultures, from which most of us have descended (Deut. 18:9-14).

3) **The anointing of Christ** and His powerful ministry compared with us our present large "L" for "Learner" plates. He was indeed anointed with power from above (more than) His partners (Heb. 1:9).

4) The meaning of Jesus' words, "...**greater works than these will he (who believes) do,** because I go to the Father" (John 14:12).

5) A comparison of the former and latter outpourings of the Holy Spirits (Joel 2:23).

6) The moment NOW in God's **progressive revelation** of HIS unfolding will, as this Age draws to a close.

7) The need for **the church to be totally cleansed by deliverance etc.** that the withered, sick old lady may become a beautiful Bride for Christ, without spot or blemish (Eph. 5:25- 27, 2 Peter 3:14).

Are we arguing the Bible away? No, we are endeavouring to understand it. The big question you may raise is: *"What support do the scriptures give to continuous ministry of deliverance and healing?"* Or, to put it another way: "Why do some people appear to be healed progressively over a period of months-even years, when the Bible speaks constantly of instantaneous or immediate healings?"

Let us answer this question one step at a time.

(i) "TIME" IN BIBLICAL NARRATIVE.

The notion that the New Testament presents us with a series of immediate healings and deliverances is, at the very least, highly questionable. Both deliverances and healings were not ALWAYS speedily concluded by a single word of command, although we usually understand the narrative that way **because of the truncated or brief record of the incidents.** For example, it is widely believed that the sermons of the apostles are recorded only in note form as the Holy Spirit brought to Luke's mind ONLY the essentials of their messages for the New Testament record. One can read Peter's sermon on the Day of Pentecost in approximately *three and a half minutes* and we are told that it resulted in three thousand conversions. I do not think any Bible student seriously takes the view that Peter preached such a short sermon.

In various places the record of the passage of time creates some difficulties e.g. Jesus' "short" prayer in the Garden of Gethsemane (Mark 14:35-41, Matt. 26:39-45). It takes **ten seconds** to read the prayer from the New Testament but Jesus apparently prayed for approximately **three hours.** Again it is a case of the bare details and principles of the actual incident being recorded for our benefit and it is very difficult to gauge the actual time elapsing without textual evidence. Similarly it is very difficult to gauge the time that deliverances and healings took to accomplish as **the New Testament record of each incident is brief and to the point.** The bare facts are given in almost log-book style. Consider for a moment the very heart of the New Testament, the Crucifixion of the Lord. How do the New Testament writers treat the actual crucifixion itself? If you or I had been eye–witnesses to the event, we would probably have written a book, or at least a chapter, on the details of the nailing to, and the erection of, the Cross, but as **Arthur Katz** points out, the Holy Spirit records it all in stark brevity - "and they crucified Him."

At least ten dramatic minutes, recorded in FOUR words. We err greatly if we assume that all the incidents in the gospel narratives were instantaneous happenings, unless they are specifically recorded as such.

(II) PRINCIPLES OF WARFARE FROM THE OLD TESTAMENT

The deliverance ministry has often been compared to the children of Israel's invasion of the Promised Land. Sometimes it appears there are giants in the Land (Numb. 13:30f) and the faint-hearted are afraid to tackle the enemy because they do not really believe God's Word that they are to go in and possess it because it is given to them (Numb. 13:2, Josh. 1:3). Even though the Land was given to them by the promise of God, they still had to go in and claim it; fight for it, if necessary (Deut. 7:16-18). It is therefore interesting to note that Moses goes on to say: **"And the Lord your God will cast out those nations before you little by little;** you may not consume them at once lest the beasts[1] of the fields increase upon you" (Deut. 7:22, cf. Exod. 23:29-33). Here is an amazing explanation for the GRADUAL entry into victory by the Jews against their enemies. **The enemy were to be dispossessed "little by little"** and this would work to the benefit of God's people. So it is with casting out demons today. **Quick and easy victories produce smugness and carelessness which prove our eventual undoing.** Victories we have to fight for are cherished, and ground won is held jealously and tenaciously. Thus our Christian armour is always "on" and every counter-attack to

---

1   Please study "Creation spirits" Book 1. Chapter 3.

devour us (like beasts of the field) comes to nothing. Indeed, there are many similarities between the warfare conducted by Joshua in the Old Testament and the warfare conducted by Jesus today, as can be seen in the comparison table (next page). If indeed it is true that the battles engaged in by Joshua and the Jews to enter Canaan and overcome its inhabitants are a type or forerunner of the **spiritual** battles we read of in the New Testament, and experience today in deliverance work, then this is solid evidence for continuous deliverance today, obtaining gradual results - battle by battle - until the war is won in our souls and we are truly filled with the Holy Spirit continuously.

(iii) PRINCIPLES OF WARFARE FROM THE NEW TESTAMENT

(a) EXAMPLES OF CONTINUOUS WARFARE

1) Legion

The removing of the kingdoms of the spirit of Legion is one of three incidents recorded in some detail in the New Testament and it is reasonable to assume that they are given as **keys to enable us to understand how the ministry of deliverance was generally conducted.**

a) This incident, when all three gospels are harmonised, indicates a persistent attempt by Legion to avoid serious disadvantage, i.e.

     i.   not to be tormented (Mark 5:7, Luke 8:28)
    ii.   not to be sent out of the country (Mark 5:10)
   iii.   not to be sent into the abyss (Luke 8:31) but finally
   iv.   to be sent into the swine (Mark 5:12, Luke 8:32).

PRINCIPLES OF SPIRITUAL WARFARE

OLD TESTAMENT WARFARE	DELIVERANCE TODAY
1. The Lord's leader is named Joshua	Same -- The Lord's leader is named Jesus (Greek), which is Joshua in Hebrew.
2. The Word of God says -- it's yours - go in and take it (Deut. 2:24, Josh. 1:1-9)	The Word of God says-- "I give you authority ...over all the power of the enemy." (Luke 10:19, cf. Matt.28:18-20)
3. But the victory has to be claimed and won (Deut. 2:24)	Same -- Luke 10:17)
4. **Unclean kingdoms of flesh are driven out** (Deut. 2:36, Josh. 23:9-10)	**Unclean kingdoms of spirit are driven out** (Matt. 12:24-28)
5. There may be some failures (Josh. 15:63,16:10,17:12-13)	Same -- see Chapter 9, Book 3 (Mark 9:28)
6. Making deals with the enemy causes problems (Josh. 9, 23:12-13)	Same -- see Chapter 1, "Exorcism" Book 1
7. The enemy tries deception in order to stay put (Josh. 9)	Same -- compare the occult woman with the spirit of a python (Acts 16:16-18, cf. Mark 1:23-27)
8 Gradual victories work out for the best. Speedy victories make us vulnerable to further attacks (Deut. 7:22)	Same -- study this chapter carefully and compare Deut. 7 and the ten lepers (Luke 17:11-19, nine of whom were ungrateful

All this took place (together with the question of name) AFTER the command to come out of the man (Luke 8:28-32, Mark 5:6-13), indicating **drawn-out opposition to the command of the Lord. Legion did NOT leave at the first word of command!** How long did all the arguing take? The answer is that we don't know, but the point is that overcoming opposition or engaging in dialogue takes TIME. Such was their rebellious nature that, even though they knew that they must bow the knee to the Holy One of Israel and depart in due course, they hung onto their dwelling-place as long as possible, whilst pleading for their immediate future.

b) Matthew 8:31 uses a verb in the imperfect tense which gives the meaning "the demons besought Him *continuously"* or **"kept begging Him,"** as Father Lazarus Moore translates the phrase for the Russian Orthodox Church (Abroad). **The same repetition** is indicated in Mark's account (5:10). It is reasonable to assume that any spirit which argues the case with the Lord Jesus Christ before obeying His direct command is going to give any disciple (learner) a hard time. The "single command" theory cannot be sustained from the account of the deliverance of the man with the Legion, and indeed all the evidence points to a full-scale deliverance session.

c) It is also interesting to note that **Kenneth Hagin** in his book, **"I Believe in Visions,"** recounts an encounter with Jesus in which the Lord explains some of the difficulties of His clash with Legion. While I do not take my stand on Kenneth Hagin's (or anybody else's) visions (Col. 2:18), it nevertheless confirms my understanding of Legion's rebellion, viz.:

> "Jesus said to Kenneth Hagin,
> ...'to cast them out you sometimes have to know not only **the kind of spirit** but also **their name** and **number.** Notice when dealing with the man from Gadara, I said, come out of this man thou unclean spirit, *but he didn't come out.'*

> 'This was something I had completely overlooked in this

Scripture before, but on re-reading the fifth chapter of Mark I noticed that this was true. He (Jesus) asked him, 'What is thy name'? And he answered, saying, 'My name is Legion; for we are many'." (Mark 5:9)

2) The Epileptic ("I Believe in Visions" p.79)

Similarly another detailed case of Jesus performing deliverance is the deaf and dumb epileptic boy, wherein Mark 9:26 employs the use of **"polla"** so that **Father Lazarus** (who has ministered deliverance himself) translates this in context as "(convulsing) **repeatedly."** This gives us the clue to **a rather more prolonged deliverance than appears at first sight** because the repeated convulsions took place AFTER Jesus commands the spirits to leave (v. 25). Perhaps if the ruling spirit had left with all its workers in a single explosive moment the cure may well have been more damaging than the infirmity, but this was not so.

It would be fair to say that on a practical level there are many people receiving ministry who could not cope with a speedy deliverance. They have jobs to keep and homes to run, and to have a significant part of their personality torn down (even though it is anti-Christ) could be quite a shattering experience if it were to happen too quickly. **Progressive deliverance gives time for the new creature to emerge and adjust** to the many changes taking place, and to the increase of the Holy Spirit within.

The Lord knows what is best for each one of us. *New life-styles* have to be learned according to the New Covenant of the Lord Jesus Christ, and a *new discipline (discipleship)* of attending to Bible study, prayers and Christian fellowship has to be encouraged in people to whom all the kinds of things that many Christians take for granted are brand-new, and even revolutionary. We should ponder on the fact that *Jesus' ministry was to the congregation of Israel - steeped in God's Word and already under tight religious discipline, but today* **we often minister to people to whom submission, commitment,**

obedience and discipline are almost unknown, and they have an enormous task before them - learning to put away their old impulsive and rebellious habits and life-style altogether, and to put to death (to crucify) the flesh, the old man (nature) and his ways. This takes time and patience and the good Lord knows the frailty of our frame, hence gradual deliverance gives an opportunity to taste of praise, worship, fellowship and teaching in **gentle stages of growing and consolidating** so that eventually the child of God has negotiated a stunning transition from one who *receives* ministry to one who *gives* out to others. Some are quick - some are slow - God knows best. Too many ministries today think their job is done as soon as *one* spirit is removed - that is deception!

The point we make here is that no one can say (from the narrative) the length of time indicated by the "convulsing repeatedly" in Mark 9:26, except to say that it was NOT instantaneous.

Fasting takes time

It should also be borne in mind that the disciples failed in ministering to this case and Jesus himself said that **"this kind cannot be driven out by anything but prayer and fasting."** *It is apparent that prayer and fasting can only be effected over a protracted period of time.* Clearly there are some spirits that are so tenacious in maintaining the gates of the fortress of hades that Christians *will find it necessary to prepare themselves for a campaign* by prayer and fasting if they are to prevail, and this MAY ALSO include the subject receiving ministry.

3) The Python.
In the same hour

The only apostolic deliverance given in some small detail is the case of the woman with **the spirit of the python** (divination) which came out *in the same hour* (Acts 16:18) which, I suggest, is hardly the same as "immediately." It is a phrase used to indicate an approximate measure of time in several places in the New Testament where time in society is measured by cocks crowing or positions of the sun rather than modern clockwork precision. Further, there is a Greek word for "immediately" (sometimes translated "straightway"), the absence of which is significant when we consider that Luke uses it on seventeen other occasions, and even that word can be used in a relative sense to mean one or two days (cf. Mark 1:28).

Other instances of PROGRESSIVE healings and deliverances occur both in the scriptures and in the experiences of those practising these ministries today. Some possible scriptural examples are Eutychus (Acts 20:9-12) and the blind man (Mark 8:22-26) while the Syrophoenician woman has to be very persistant before the barriers to the deliverance of her daughter are swept away by the Lord (Mark 7:24-30, Matt. 15: 21-28.)[1] Also many progressive healings have been recorded during the ministry of the late **Kathryn Kuhlman** ("I Believe in Miracles", pages 34-35, 80-82) and there are many testimonies of like experiences available from the Healing Ministry at St. Andrew's Cathedral Sydney, conducted by **Canon Jim Glennon** and now **Canon Jim Holbeck,** and other centres throughout the world.

b) VARIETIES OF GIFTS

1) Gifts of Healings

Gifts of Healings are listed as vaild gifts of the Holy Spirits of Christ for His body the Church in 1 Corinthians, chapter 12, and it is interesting to note that Paul (no doubt conscious of the many and various ministries operating at the time, perhaps with vastly different methodologies and emphases, yet with the essential principles of faith in Christ being honoured by the operation of the power of the Spirit) is careful not to call it a gift of healing, but *uses a double plural* "gifts of healings" (v9). So too today we observe a variety of gifts of healings emerging in

---

1   For a fuller treatment see "End-Time Deliverance."

the church from one side of the world to the other. That this plurality includes the deliverance ministry with its own variety of styles, yet with fundamental and biblical common ground, is also obvious when we observe that the deliverance weapons of **"words of knowledge," "miracles" (powers)** and **"discerning of spirits"** are also included in Paul's list of gifts in the context of the same passage. It is obvious that the operation of the gifts of words of knowledge and/or discerning spirits is essential in any effective deliverance ministry, and that **the removal of ANY spirit, whether a ruler or a worker, is a miracle,** when it is removed by the supernatural and invisible power of the Holy Spirit (Matt. 12:28).

That is a very important truth and worth reflecting on for a moment. **Every unclean spirit that is cast out is normally[1] the result of the Holy Spirit executing the commands of a deliverance minister in Jesus' Name** and because it is a spirit victory obtained by the Holy Spirit intervening in the lives of mortal or physical men and women **each removal is, by definition, a miracle.** So if you have a large group meeting where 2,000 or 3,000 spirits are removed in a couple of hours you really have a MIRACLE meeting - praise the Lord!. However most miracle chasers are not impressed by miracles they cannot see, because we now have a climate in the Renewal Church where people want to SEE physical miracles in the form of signs and wonders. We have to encourage Christians to understand that the INNER miracles taking place within the soul and mind, invisible to the human eye, are even more important than the external physical signs which the Lord is doing, for although the Kingdom of God[2] is demonstrated by signs and wonders it does not consist of physical things but "righteousness and peace and joy in the Holy Spirit" (Rom. 14:17), the INNER qualities that so many Christians do not enjoy today but should be experiencing. Physical miracles are wonderful, but they are really wonderful POINTERS (dare I say it) for the un-saved or the weak in spirit. **It is the SOULS of His**

---

1   That is, unwilling removals not caused by death.

2   More on the Kingdom of God in section (iv)

people that the Lord Jesus really wants to get started into with His cleansing grace. Was it not the Lord Himself who said that **"it is better for you to enter the Kingdom of God with one eye, than with two eyes to be thrown into Hell."** (Mark 9:47b) Ponder that saying for a moment and you will understand how much more important INNER invisible healings (deliverance) is to the Lord than external visible healings. It is more important for a soul to be clean than a body to be healed, but of course, a clean soul greatly blesses the body (Mark 2:5-12, John 5:14, Jas. 5:16).

Every deliverance is a miracle and a healing, but understandbly common usage in the Body of Christ today usually describes a healing in the SOULISH area (emotional, mental and spiritual) as a DELIVERANCE and a physical healing of the BODY (organs, flesh and bones etc.) as a HEALING. This is quite workable, so long as we do not lose sight of the fact that deliverance is a major part of the gifts of healings, and that very little, if any healing from Christ is achieved without some invisible deliverance taking place because **our warfare is ALWAYS spiritual.** (Eph. 6:12, 2Cor. 10:3-4).

The very close affinity between **preaching, healing and deliverance (casting out demons)** is evident in various parts of the ministry of Jesus, His commission to the disciples and their works as apostles; and the Holy Spirit, perhaps by knowledge or discernment, will convict us at the appropriate time as to how to minister, so as sons of God we should be open to His leading on each occasion (Rom. 8:14). As a general rule of thumb for doubtful cases (whilst experience in discernment is being obtained) a prayer of faith for body or flesh healing could be offered in the first instance. If that ministry appears to be unsuccessful it is reasonable to assume that there is SPIRITUAL resistance caused by principalities and powers (rulers and authorities) and that specific deliverance may be necessary before healing can take place (cf. spirit of infirmity - Luke 13:10 -17).

2) Discernment

When studying the deliverance of the girl with the python spirit it is worth noting that this woman followed Paul and Silas for MANY DAYS before Paul became sufficiently aware of her menace and DISCERNED the enemy within her (Acts 16:16-18). I think it is true to say that *one of the greatest single causes of delay or lack of success in the healing and deliverance ministry is inadequate discernment,* and when considering the length of time the ministry sometimes takes, discernment[1] (or lack of it) has to be taken into account. The case of one subject who came to us is typical. She suffered from a massive infection of eastern religious spirits which chattered incessantly in her head night and day and nearly drove her insane. *After they were cleaned out, other spirits were discerned,* ministered against and eliminated. She improved and was able to work again while receiving ministry for the eighth type of spirit the Lord had searched out. **Once total deliverance has been claimed by a child of God, the Spirit of God apparently does not want to cease His work until His temple is TOTALLY free.**[2] This would be the invariable experience of all our subjects, *and it takes time.*

A trap to avoid

Too often have I seen people who have not been aware of this, **break off receiving continuous deliverance ministry because they "felt better"** and thought that not only the current battle but also the whole war was over and victory was complete.[3] Medical doctors who prescibe certain courses of medicine, only to see them quickly abandoned by their patients will know the problem too well. It grieves me when a sufferer misreads the evidence and ceases ministry, usually before we have even begun to scratch the surface of the unclean empire of kingdoms within their soul. It may mean that (i) they only

---

1   See Book 1 Chapter 3 (6), Book 3, 9, 3 (ii), and Book 4.

2   See "End Time Deliverance."

3   Discussed fully in Book 3, Chap. 7 and 8, 1 (iii).

wanted a "patch-up" repair job from the Lord in order to get their lives moving again the way *THEY* want to go, and they are not really interested in what HE wants to do in their lives, or it can mean that (ii) they do not believe your counsel. All you can do (after counselling) is pray that the Lord will bring them to see what you can see and that they will return to a deliverance ministry in due course with a more patient and obedient spirit.

When we have *ALL FAITH* so as to move mountains and *ALL DISCERNMENT,* then perhaps we can expect speedy and full deliverances fairly regularly. DO YOU know of any one who has this kind of equipment from the Lord? Don't be discouraged. We are all learners and have to start somewhere. Once the good Lord sees our faith and trust (commitment) and finds us faithful in little things, He will surely entrust us with greater things in due time. Hallelujah!

3) Authority and Power[1]

We have already said a few things about these most important subjects, but not enough!

Flesh or spirit?

When immediate healings are not obtained the question often arises as to whether the ministry has been carried out **"in the flesh."** This is a phrase used by some to indicate that a ministry is proceeding with human power rather than the power of the Holy Spirit. Although this term is not used in the context of ministry in the scriptures, it perhaps is not an inappropriate description of the attempt at deliverance by the sons of Sceva (Acts 19:13–17)[2]. However there can be no parallel comparison between their ministry and that of disciples of the Lord Jesus. They use Jesus' name as a magic formula without

---

1   See "Christian Authority and Power" for a fuller treatment, also Book 1 Chap. 3 (1).
2   See Book 1, Chap. 3 (4).

knowing His Person. They neither understand His authority nor power, nor the promises of the New Covenant ratified with His precious blood. They are unregenerate or unsanctified creatures endeavouring to use holy things for advantage - children of wrath without the seal of God's Holy Spirit upon them or in them. We can say of their ministry "it is flesh" without fear of error, and they paid a price for their foolishness.

But what of the disciples? They also failed with their ministry to the deaf and dumb epileptic. Was that also of the flesh? Jesus' answer was not that they erred in ministering, or that their technique was bad or fleshly, but that they lacked FAITH. There are some spirits which necessitate that disciples prepare through **prayer and fasting** and, when the attack is pressed, **it must be pressed with all authority.**

Determination and perseverance

Flabbiness in the authority of the minister reflects flabbiness in faith, and this is exposed in any situation where tenacious, rebellious spirits of high rank are encountered. Unclean spirits are quick to discern doubt and despair in Christian soldiers, such as, "What's wrong, Lord? Why don't they obey us?" flitting across the mind and they are quick to seize any advantage. It has been said by a well-know general that the army which hangs on in the heat of the battle an extra five minutes (longer than the enemy) gains the victory. How many times in the early days of the ministry I have been on the verge of giving up (to try again another day) when a co-worker, pressing on, has to my utter delight, obtained the victory.

Feelings of the minister

Sometimes we confuse the leading of the Holy Spirit with our own enthusiasm, negativity or other emotions.[1] We cannot

---

1   This is a complex matter, and I only seek to sound a warning here. The clear leading of the Holy Spirit must be obeyed, of course. See Book 3, Chap. 8, 1 (iii).

always afford to wait until we "feel" anointed before ministering but we should act BY FAITH upon the Word and promises of God according to the need placed before us, regardless of how we "feel" in our flesh. When we act in FAITH and insist on our AUTHORITY as revealed in the Word of God, we so often find that *God supplies His anointing POWER in response to our obedience.* This is true of prayer, sermons, praise or any spiritual activity. Perhaps the spiritual principle of 1 Cor. 15:46 - "... it is not the spiritual which is first, but the physical ..." has some relevance here also, and that which begins "in the flesh" can end "in the Spirit."

Also there is a mistaken idea abroad among Christian ministers that if we are all soundly converted Christians and use the name of Jesus, everybody has the same power. The power is in the Name (they say) and each one of us Christian ministers has ALL of Christ by virtue of His Spirit indwelling us, and therefore we ALL have ALL power to do all ministries. "Failures" are then attributed to lack of faith by the subject because they have been told to believe they are healed or delivered - whether they are or not. These notions are often "religious" or presumptuous rather than accurate.

Why have some Christian ministers adopted this line of teaching? Simply because they have not understood that:

> i) Discernment of the REAL problem is often essential.
>
> ii) Some victories are not won in five minutes.
>
> iii) Some ministers are more crucified with Christ than others, and it is the measure of the anointing power of God's Spirit that is all - important.

This is best illustrated by the Church at Philadelphia to whom Jesus said, **"I know that you have but little power, and yet you have kept my Word and have not denied my Name"** (Rev. 3:8). What do we learn from this? At least two things:

i) **Little power** means exactly that. The measure of power given to one may be vastly different from the measure of power given to another.

ii) Even more surprisingly, *the measure of power granted to a minister MAY have little or no relationship to his faithfulness in keeping the Word of God and acknowledging the name of Jesus.*

Our little power

It is a grace, a gift and cannot be earned - although we know that the Lord honours faithfulness, and the Name of Jesus and the Word of God are essentials in any effective ministry. If it were possible to line up ten ministers who believe with equal force and enthusiasm in the power of Jesus' Name and the authority of the Bible **each one would exhibit different levels of POWER** in their preaching, deliverance and healing ministries. Otherwise preachers and teachers of the Bible with Ph.D's and Masters degrees in Theology would have all the most powerful ministries, but **the Lord usually works it the other way around.** Not many mighty are chosen for His mighty works (1 Cor. 1:26).

The Lord may entrust His power to a person of simple and honest faithfulness while the learned theologian, who can translate freely from the Hebrew and Greek scriptures into other languages receives, like the Philadelphians, but little power. Obviously it is a question of different gifts and roles of service and we must use whatever gifts we are given so that "to him who has, more shall be given to him, in abundance, but whosoever has not, even that which he has shall be taken away" (Matt. 25:14-30). So it is not so much a matter of how MUCH we KNOW (with our minds) but what is our particular ANOINTING from the Lord, and its measure. I believe **the measure of our anointing is directly related to our personal level of crucifixion with Christ** (Philip. 3:10).

It is obvious that without a full measure of power (literally "dynamite") of the Spirit any ministry will fall short of the New Testament model, for "the Power of the Lord was with Him (Jesus) to heal" (Luke 5:17). I have nearly always felt I needed more power from the Lord. Even as I write this, my own inadequacy burdens me. When I visit the market place and see people in wheelchairs with shrivelled limbs or spastics and mongoloids being led around by devoted parents I feel even more impotent, but I am comforted by the Lord because I know that the day of Power is coming. If you, too have little power, do what the Philadelphians did! Minister His Word in His Name, but let us also seek to deepen our relationship with Christ by truly putting to death the desires of our flesh and then become more available and usable for HIS purposes.

However let me add that, especially in the ministry of deliverance, I believe we should minister to the needy and say little or nothing about results - that is not our job or prerogative. Let us minister by faith and let the Lord teach us and bring forth fruit from His Word and ministry. Let us who minister not make presumptuous or grandiose claims because, in God's perfect timing, testimonies of the goodness of our God will flow *from those who are delivered and healed.*

The Lord will not see you put to shame but He who sees the true motives of your heart will vindicate your faithfulness in due time and an open door will be put before you (Rev. 3:7-8). Praise the Lord! However, while it is obvious that every gift or talent from God must be put to use if it is to be increased and bring pleasure to the donor (Matt. 25:14-30), we will always be in the position where we need to be *utterly dependant upon the grace and anointing of God* for every challenging moment, in the ministries of Deliverance and Healing.

(c) GUIDELINES FOR SUFFERERS MINISTERING TO OTHERS

Somewhere in our training the question always arises "How clean do you have to be before you can minister (deliverance) to others?"

That is a good question. Let us look at the two extremes in order to arrive at the mind of Christ in this.

Extreme No. 1

Do you know anyone perfect, that is, perfectly clean? No sin disease of the heart, no death in them? **Of course you don't** (I John 1:7-9). Therefore if the Lord were to wait until His servants were perfectly clean before they ministered deliverance to others there would be no ministry at all. Obviously the Lord uses imperfect (polluted) vessels all the time.

Extreme No. 2

A woman who has been a practising witch for twenty years is recently converted to Jesus Christ and joins your church. Because of her total involvement, enthusiasm and keenness in spiritual things she wants to lay hands on the sick. Do you let her? **Of course you don't,** because although she has been greatly blessed, she is still far too much of a mixture, and likely to minister with soul power rather than the Holy Spirit.[1]

Obviously the way to go is to allow only those people who have a discernible measure of the following qualities to minister to others in your flock:

1.   Soundly converted to Christ.
2.   A basic knowledge of the Word of God.
3.   Learning and practising true discipleship.
4.   Submitted to your authority.
5.   Showing some fruit of the Spirit.
6.   Living and moving in the Spirit most of the time.

Even when you select your "best" people to serve the Lord as deliverance ministers or counsellors you can be sure that somewhere along the way the Lord will want to give them a

---

1   See Book 1 (3rd Ed.) Chap. 3,6 (ii) (a) "Beware the Counterfeit".

good clean–out also, and that could lead to a lengthy season of cleansing for them.[1]

Our present practice

As our anointing has increased, so also we have found that we need the assistance of counsellors less and less. Indeed the Power of God takes care of the otherwise dramatic cases and those who would have been counsellors in the old days are now themselves receiving continuous Deliverance and Restoration, in preparation for the coming of the Bridegroom (Eph. 5:25-27, 2 Peter 3:14).

The guidelines we now give the people in our Deliverance and Restoration program stress that only our Deacons are permitted to minister to those in OUR program, when Verlie and myself are not available.

However, as so many in our program are full-on disciples of Jesus, and have totally surrendered to Him their spirit, soul and body (1 Thess. 5:23) - thoroughly taught by the Word and strong in Spirit of God, they are free to minister to others OUTSIDE our program as the Lord leads them.[2] Here are our present guidelines TO THOSE IN OUR PROGRAM:

Guidelines for Those Ministering to Others

1. Freely minister deliverance to those OUTSIDE our program who ask for or need urgent help.

Generally speaking, the principles are to:

(i)   BIND non-Christians rather than risk worsening their condition (Matt. 12:43-45).

(ii) Loose Christians or believers (Matt. 15:22-28).

---

1   See Chapter 5.12 Authority and Teamwork 10.

2   See Book 1, Chapter 3,1 "Who May Cast Out".

2. **Please do not minister deliverance to those within our program, except in an emergency.**

   (i)   It is essential that you do you NOT cut across the main weekly ministry and its discernment.

   (ii) Please realise that INTERCESSION is continuing throughout the week for ALL in the program.

   (iii) Beware guessing and naming unclean spirits, thereby causing confusion, extending suffering, despair and wasting the intercession.

   - in a word, beware creating DISUNITY of ministry - this plays into the enemy's hands.

3. **Emergency ministry to those in the program.**

   (i)   To avoid confusion with the main ministry do not risk naming the unclean spirit. Say *"You have been commanded and named, you unclean spirits. Loose him/her in Jesus Name"* - or something similar.

   (ii) Loose - do not bind. If you bind what the ministers are loosing every week you will be in conflict with the main ministry and doing the sufferer a disservice.

   (iii) Inform the Pastor or Deliverance Minister of the emergency and your actions as soon as possible, for either confirmation or further action.

4. **Emergency ministry is RARELY necessary,** because of the ongoing authority that applies 24 hours a day from the main ministry program on Sundays.

Every week the unclean is commanded to go "during all Christian activity". This means that it only takes the hearing or the reading of the Word of God, listening to praise tapes or prayer, for a short season, to obtain the loosing required.

(iv) THE KINGDOM OF GOD

(a) DEFINITION

It is widely accepted in biblical circles that the phrase **"Kingdom of God:** is synonymous with **"Kingdom of Heaven,"** because devout Jews, reluctant to use the term "God" for fear of blaspheming by using it flippantly, substitute the word "Heaven" in order to overcome their religious sensitivity. It is also understood that "kingdom" means "rule," so that **"the Kingdom of God"** does not refer simply to a geographical area but wherever **God's rule,** order or authority is set up over sin or pollution of any kind. Thus the Kingdom of God can manifest itself anywhere.

(b) THE KINGDOM OF GOD AND DELIVERANCE

When Jesus was challenged by the Pharisees with using the power of Beelzebub, the Prince of demons, His reply included the phrase, **"If I by the Spirit of God cast out demons, then is the Kingdom of God come upon you."** That is to say, the rule of God has displaced the rule of satan whenever demons are cast out (Matt. 12:26-28). What a glorious description and vindication of the deliverance ministry are these words of the Lord!

Bread ministry

Did you know that the deliverance ministry is **Christ's BREAD**[1] **for the people of God?** Jesus says this plainly in the incident with the Greek (Syrophoenician) woman. She is a Canaanitish (idolatrous, occult) woman who beseeches the Lord to deliver

---

1   See Book 1, Chapter 2.6 (vi).

her severely demonised daughter but because of the historical time slot of this incident (between the Testaments[1]) Jesus declared that His ministry is primarily for the Jews and it is not proper to minister to the Gentiles (yet). He says **"It is not well to take the children's (Israel's) bread and throw it to the dogs (Gentiles),"** but her answer is full of faith, **"Yes Lord, (but) even the dogs eat from the crumbs which fall from their master's table"** (Mark 7:24-30, Matt. 15:21-28).

She does not ask for the children's bread but only for the crumbs! Such is her faith in the Lord Jesus, she perceives that the deliverance of her daughter would be but a small demonstration (crumbs) of His total Saviourhood and that He is not only Master (Lord) of the Jews but of the Gentiles also!

If you are one of the those Christian leaders who has always believed that a Christian could not have a demon may I ask you to consider carefully this incident of deliverance?

Deliverance is a BREAD[2] ministry. That is to say it is a provision which comes from the "Living Bread" Himself and it must not be withheld from the children of God. Who are the children of God today? Israelites? Christians? Both? Certainly Born Again Christians know they are God's children and should freely receive Bread ministries such as deliverance without traditional doctrines getting in the way. If this incident teaches us anything at all it is that Deliverance is not normally for unbelievers but **it is for believers!**

---

1   That is, at the end of the Old Testament Age and just prior to the beginning of the New Testament Age which begins at the Cross, when the veil in the Temple was torn from top to bottom (Matt. 27:50-51).

2   I AM INDEBTED FOR THIS INSIGHT TO SIMON CANT (20) WHO HAD ALREADY MOVED INTO MINISTERING GROUP DELIVERANCE. IT SEEMS THAT WHEN "MATURE" CHRISTIANS HANG BACK FROM THE BATTLE THE LORD IS OBLIGED TO USE GRANDMOTHERS, HOUSEWIVES AND YOUNG MEN BARELY OUT OF THEIR TEENS.

Traditional errors

The Bible says that all we Christian teachers make many mistakes (James 3:1-2), It is not that we plan to or want to, but simply that our understanding of the mind of Christ is limited or incomplete and we are not always able to see what the Word of God is really saying. **Traditional interpretations of men have somehow been interwoven with the Word deep within our understanding,** and firmly lodged in our memory banks. It seems to me that if the Lord is now pouring out a continuous flow of revelational knowledge to His people, many of our time-honoured interpretations will need to be amended or even thrown out to make way for the fresh light that is coming from the Lord, and this applies to the "big" ministries just as much as the "little" ministries.

There are many great ministries in the world on the international preaching and healing circuit, with powerful anointings on them, which still have not come to terms with the truth that born- again, tongue-speaking Christians can be and are severely demonised, and this traditional teaching is unfortunately holding up the vast majority of Christians from moving into God's full salvation for them, i.e., their full restoration into the image of the Son of God by means of **individual** and **group** inner cleansing and purification.

The children's bread is (unintentionally?) being kept from them, so how can they get cleaned up and make themselves ready for the Bridegroom? The truth of the matter is that as well as all the wonderful things that the Lord is doing in and through the Church, satan has been and continues to be busy also. Many "members" of the Church of God who are hoping to be part of the Bride are living lives of terrible conflict. Such have been the inroads of millions of demons into the lives of Christians, both by hereditary factors and the evil and adulterous generation in which we live, that the lives of many "Christians" are indistinguishable from the pagans around them. They gluttonise, fornicate, commit adultery, lie, cheat, steal, take drugs, deceive and even blaspheme. In many cases they do *NOT* want to do these things and **ANYONE who tells them that they do not, indeed cannot, have a demon is robbing them of their bread (full salvation)** available from Christ. Indeed the error is horrendously destructive because it is satan's major philosophical stand and bulwark against both individual Christians and the corporate Body of Christ, that is, against all those who desire to be transformed and RESTORED into the image of the Son of God **prior** to the Rapture (1 Thess. 4:16-17, 2 Peter 3:14).

Word ministry

If the Church Bride is to become beautiful she must make herself ready and be cleansed, purified, purged and restored by the washing of water with the Word (Eph. 5:26).

Deliverance is a Word ministry that distinguishes between spirit and soul, good and evil, Holy and unclean, and brings an increase of the Rule of God within us. In the face of all detractors and critics, Jesus says to the Pharisees (today's and yesterday's) that if it is true that we cast out demons by the *Spirit of God* then in the very act of DISPLACEMENT of the unclean spirits by the Holy Spirit, the RULE OF GOD comes upon those involved. There are not too many ministries around of which that can be said with such confidence, but effective evangelism, deliverance and healing – the three essential ministries of a full salvation certainly qualify.

This kingdom or rule of God in and over the human heart, soul, mind and body obviously increases step by step as unclean spirits are cast out and the Holy Spirit is prayed in, and this suggests **a progressive growth of the Kingdom of God in us**. The question is, is this consistent with the scriptures? The next section will show that it is.

(c) THE KINGDOM OF GOD AND GROWTH

The New Testament tells us that **the Kingdom of God "is like**

a grain of mustard seed, which when it is sown upon the earth, though it is less than all the seeds that are upon the earth, yet when it is sown, it GROWS UP and becomes greater than all the herbs, and it puts out great branches, so that the birds of heaven are able to dwell under its shade" (Mark 4:30-32, cf. Matt. 13:31-32).

It is plain that God's rule with the mustard seed has been one of growth - so slow that it is imperceptible to the human eye yet nevertheless so constant and real that what God created as very tiny, progresses into a tree. **The mustard seed is used as a parable to describe faith** (Matt. 17:20), the kind of faith that can move mountains. Faith can be very small, even tiny like that of a mustard seed, but *when even tiny faith is placed in Jesus* it can achieve great things because the rule of God is established where there is faith in Christ. It is not so much the SIZE of your faith but the OBJECT in which you place your faith (Jesus) which causes growth. Therefore **the rule or Kingdom of God is a continuously growing Kingdom today within the faithful disciple(s) of Jesus.**

As faith brings you deliverance and satan's kingdom is banished so the rule of God comes more and more upon you as the object of His grace - sometimes quickly and suddenly - sometimes slowly as a matter of constant growth. **Jesus described this gradual progression as "first the blade, then the ear, then the full grain in the ear"** Mark 4:28.

Thus deliverance, which brings the Kingdom of God upon us, is necessarily progressive in its effect and visibility, that is its fruit-bearing, as "we are being changed from one degree of glory to another" (2 Cor. 3:18).

(v) CONCLUSION

I think it needs to be said that **whether deliverances and/or healings happen quickly or slowly, there is no way every observer is going to be satisfied.** The Lord Jesus exercised a dynamic ministry in the power of the Spirit and yet He had legions of critics (cf. John 15:23-25). It is hard for the traditionalist, indeed any of us, to kick against the goads (Acts 26:14) - Saul even had to be blinded for three days to show him real darkness, and to draw his attention to his true spiritual state. He loved the Word of God as much as any true Christian, but his traditional background blinded him to the truth of a God who was (and is) on the move! Is this not true of many traditional Christians today?

What we have said about the Kingdom of God and its continuous growth should be the normal situation for every Christian who is abiding in the Word of God and living the life of a true disciple. We all know that one never stands still in life, whatever our field of endeavour. We either go forward or we go backwards and it is no different in our spiritual lives. We either go forward into the unsearchable riches of Christ or we drift into forgetfulness, becoming dull of hearing and blurred of sight as we allow the flesh to overtake the spirit.

Growing as a Christian

If we are one of those who stay close to God, continuously learning new things from His Word and being led by His Spirit, there will be a continuous release taking place in our lives, freeing us from the things of the world more and more. This is normally thought of as "growing in grace", sanctification or "Christian maturity" and it is a most important aim for the sincere Christian. We ALL ought to aim for this continuous increase of the Kingdom of God in our lives because as it takes place the kingdom of satan is diminished within us.

Thus it is true every Christian who is increasing in the true knowledge and things of God is probably experiencing some spiritual release from satan and his powers of darkness, and is therefore obtaining a measure of an invisible deliverance, whether or not the specific ministry of deliverance is invoked or commanded.

Many times I have sat in church assemblies where the praise

of God has brought down the power of the Holy spirit and hundreds of "invisible" deliverances have been taking place all around me. On one occasion a pastor was preaching an inspired sermon and the power of God fell, making everyone in the assembly feel drowsy. He stopped in the middle of his message and said, "My what a sleepy lot you are today. Did you all have late nights?" not realising it had nothing to do with the flesh but was of the Spirit of God! They were all set up for a mighty outpouring of deliverance and healing, had the preacher been aware of what was happening and how to proceed. What a lot we have yet to learn. There is still a long way to go for each and every one of us who seeks to serve the Lord in this End-Time.

Forty Years

However, beware a temptation! Praise, worship, preaching and other New Testament ministries may change our lives dramatically **over the span of a life-time** and bring to us a MEASURE of deliverance by removing worker-class and, perhaps, even some middle-class spirits but they **can never take the place of specific, anointed deliverance** ministry. And today, of course, there is no more time to play games. It is time to be delivered of rulers and authorities, and quickly too. **There is no time left to take 40 years to become like Jesus!**

If we can accept that the increase of the Kingdom of God in our hearts and lives is an imperceptible, invisible, continuous increase, and also recognise that deliverance brings the Kingdom of God upon us, according to the Word of God, then it seems to me that the idea of receiving continuous deliverance should pose no problem to any thoughtful Christian, especially now that the deliverance ministry can be combined with normal worship, teaching and fellowship in your meetings.

You may not be able to accept all the evidence presented here, but its presentation will be considered worthwhile if you are brought to the point where you can say, "Fast or slow, bless your people, Lord - do it YOUR way. Increase YOUR rule in our lives - have your own way!" After twenty years of experience I'm going to stick my spiritual neck out and say that **continuous ministry is necessary for God's people everywhere if the Bride of Christ is to be thoroughly cleansed, prepared and beautiful, ready for the Bridegroom**[1] The only way I can foresee continuous ministry being unnecessary in these last days is if, in the gracious provision of the Lord, He anoints and empowers various ministers of every nation, tribe and tongue, to minister total and immediate cleansing. *Many have thought they were doing this,* but the truth is **we have had no real concept of the magnitude of the task or the meaning of the WHOLE COSMOS lying in the power of the evil one** (1 John 5:19) and therefore many have been deceived in the past. However, do not be discouraged at this for greater the task, then the greater the salvation provided by our Lord Jesus. Obviously the greater the Lord's Salvation, the greater the glory for the Godhead and the greater joy we can have as we are called to be the earthen vessels through which the Holy Spirit will achieve the great Salvation of God, which the whole Earth shall see. Hallelujah!

EPILOGUE

I do hope you will now go on to read and study carefully **Book 3 - "WALKING IN VICTORY"** (or, if that is unavailable, a smaller booklet entitled **"Guidance for Those Receiving Deliverance"),** because not only does it deal with "Opposition" (which is inevitable) but also contains a chapter with the rather quaint but meaningful title **"You've won a battle, but the *WAR* goes on".** A proposed index of Book 3 can be found under "Appendix H".

Reluctant as I am to "push" our own publications I have to tell you that I consider Books 1 and 3 are essential reading if you hope to be truly effective in Deliverance ministry, and not just a superficial "showman". Book 3 will help you to cope with the

---

1   Discussed fully in "End-Time Deliverance."

enormous pressures that come upon a Deliverance minister by warning you beforehand from which areas you can expect problems and attacks, and their nature.

Fore-warned is fore-armed. May the Lord Jesus richly bless you as you ponder on the truths contained in this series.

APPENDIX G

APPLICATION FOR DISTANT MINISTRY

Sample letter to enquirers requesting "Ministry at a Distance"

Dear Christian Enquirer,

Ministry at a Distance

In this letter we address all those Christians who are interested in receiving Christ's ministry of deliverance but who cannot physically be present at an anointed ministry for that purpose each week.

We would like you to consider being included in our "Ministry at a Distance" program. But first, two matters. Deliverance ministry is for CHRISTIANS, so if you are in any doubt about your standing in or relationship with Christ Jesus, do write and let us know. We will be only too happy to help you make sure that you ARE a Christian.

Secondly this program is for Christians who for one reason or another, are "unattached" to a Pastor and therefore cannot obtain ministry in the normal way. However we will not normally refuse ministry to anyone, attached or otherwise, who needs our help, by the grace of the Lord.

Great things are happening at Crows Nest, Sydney. Christians are being RENEWED and RESTORED. God is working by His Spirit in the innermost parts of those present in our meetings and it is showing on the outside, with growths appearing and dropping off, bones (including facial bones) being re-structured and all kinds of infirmities and sinful habits dropping away as the causal spirits are removed by deliverance in Jesus' Name.

For the vast majority of us it is not an instant ministry transformation; that would be unappreciated and of limited long-term blessing because it would not require faith and obedience over the long course. We are talking about TRANSFORMING, not COSMETIC ministry. It is a ministry where the Holy Spirit searches us out deep within, where only He can see the real problems, and this is not done in 5 minutes or even 5 hours or 5 days but over a period of time so that He can dig deeper and deeper - relentlessly, thoroughly and effectively cleansing out soul and body so that we can be TRULY and FULLY filled with the Holy Spirit, not just "topped up", as often happens today.

This ministry is not just for people who live in Sydney and can get to the meetings, but we have included Christians in Queensland, Victoria, Canberra, Newcastle[1] and even England, America, the Philippines, India and South Africa, and I am delighted to be able to say that the results are just as encouraging as for those who can attend.

However **"Ministry-at-a-Distance" people do have some obstacles to overcome** which requires their personal discipline.

Disadvantages

They don't receive the same fellowship and face-to-face encouragement that those physically present at the meetings receive, but this can partly be overcome by tapes and letters. Also they need to be able to separate themselves privately at the same time as the Sunday meeting is being held (2.30 - 5.00 p.m. Sydney time). However so long as the fairly simple guidance of the ministry is followed carefully, THE SAME RESULTS CAN BE ACHIEVED because the Lord is not limited by time or space. So you can be with us at Crows Nest in spirit, if not in the flesh, and the Holy Spirit will minister to you right where you are - because you will be "in spirit" with Him!

---

1 However we have some folk who regularly travel the 150 kms. from Newcastle, and back again EVERY Sunday (i.e. 300 kms), and from Nowra, which is even further away.

For you to be included we require four things from you, which are:-

(1) That you please read, check with the scriptures and UNDERSTAND the enclosed extract from CHRISTIAN DELIVERANCE BOOK 2 which explains distant and proxy ministry.[1]

(2) YOU SET ASIDE THE TIME BETWEEN 2.30 - 500 p.m. EACH SUNDAY (SYDNEY TIME) to be alone, if possible, and play Christian music tapes of worship and ministry (especially from our own meetings), if possible.

(3) YOU BE IN CLOSE SPIRITUAL COMMUNION WITH THE LORD, EITHER BY singing choruses, reading the Scriptures, praying, or listening to these things for the period of the meetings, along with the tapes mentioned above, and thus KEEPING YOUR SPIRIT ON JESUS as much as possible throughout.

It's okay to go under the power of God, of course, indeed it will minister to you, so don't fight any sense of "drowsiness" but flow with the Lord in this.

(4) YOU COME IN TO THE MEETING IF AT ALL POSSIBLE, or make contact by phone, letter or whatever every 4-6 weeks so we can monitor your progress and continue to include you in our regular prayers for the next month.

If there is anything else you need to know please ask. When you are ready to proceed please fill in and return the application form below together with your confidential letter explaining the areas in your life for which you desire ministry.

---

1   Feel free to photocopy the appropriate pages of this book to assist your ministry.

150

Wishing you the Lord's wisdom and guidance as you go forward in His Name.

Yours in Christ Jesus,
(Rev.) Peter Hobson.

P.S. Folk on the other side of the world may find they will be asleep during the meeting time in Sydney. Conditions (2) and (3) above are waived in such cases.

APPLICATION FOR DISTANT MINISTRY

I would like to receive deliverance and healing ministry every Sunday between 2.30 and 5.00 p.m. (Sydney time) and agree to the conditions advised by the Ministers of Full Salvation Fellowship in their accompanying letter.

NAME : ....

ADDRESS : ....

PHONE : ....

AGREEMENT

I understand that failure to contact the Fellowship for two (2) calendar months automatically discharges the ministers from their spiritual obligations to me.

(SIGNED) .... DATE ....

Because "Distant Ministry" requires a greater discipline by sufferers in that they are required to "tune in" to our Sunday meetings without the advantage of regular teaching, fellowship and encouragement from others receiving ministry, it is necessary before the close of each calendar year, for this application to be renewed by sufferers for the new year of ministry coming up.

It is important that sufferers indicate that they wish to maintain their interest and involvement fairly regularly, so that we who minister know where we stand and don't have our time and spiritual energy wasted.

We should be prepared to help those who are co-operating fully with the ministry all we can, but unfortunately there will always be those people who want the blessings of Christ without putting in the necessary effort or making the necessary sacrifices of time and obedience themselves.

A renewal of ministry letter could read something like this:-

GREETING IN JESUS' NAME

As the year of 1993 draws to a close it is a good time for us all to take a spiritual stock-take of ourselves and the progress or otherwise of our Christian walk. This is especially true for those who have requested distant ministry, because you do not have the advantages of regular fellowship, teaching and monitoring of your progress in the same way as those who can be physically present.

Because of the greater discipline necessary with distant ministry and also because the ministers' need to conserve and concentrate their spiritual resources in order to obtain, by the grace of the Lord, the best results, we ask for a RECOMMITMENT each year from those who would like to continue on.

Please read the enclosed information very carefully and ensure that you can fulfil the conditions required, before responding. This is not a ministry to be entered into lightly, but requires your consistent and full co-operation. If in doubt - DON'T.

We realise, of course, that circumstances can change and should you make a renewed start with us and want to pull out later you have only to let us know.

There is no charge for the ministry of course, but from time to time, necessary tapes will be produced and sent to you, which will assist your involvement on Sunday afternoon, for which donations are welcome, according to your ability.

Prayerfully Yours,

APPENDIX "H"

PROPOSED CONTENTS OF BOOK 3:

"WALKING IN VICTORY"

CHAPTER 7.   YOU'VE WON A BATTLE, BUT THE WAR GOES ON

1.   Battle Tactics

2.   What the afflicted can do to help

3.   Teaching
     (i) The Word
          (a) Victory
          (b) In Christ
          (c) Faith
          (d) Victory Promises
     (ii) Keeping their Deliverance and the Covenant
          (a) Relapses
          (b) Human Will
          (c) Causes
          (d) The Solution
          (e) Application
          (f) The New Covenant
     (iii) Prayer
          (a) Forgiveness
          (b) Lordship
          (c) Filled with the Spirit
          (d) The Blood of the Passover Lamb
          (e) Pray in the Spirit
     (iv) Fellowship
          (a) Worship
          (b) Sharing
          (c) Conduct
          (d) Permission to visit other Fellowships
          (e) Discretion

CHAPTER 8. OPPOSITION

1. Opposing the Sufferer
   - (i) Opposition within the World
   - (ii) Opposition within the Church
   - (iii) Opposition within themselves
     - (a) Understanding emotions
     - (b) Assessing progress
     - (c) Ensuring a good testimony
     - (d) Soulish Warfare
     - (e) A Common Deception

2. Opposition to the Minister
   - (i) Reaction of the world - Commercial interests
   - (ii) Reaction of the Church
     - (a) The Multitudes
     - (b) Friends and/or Relatives
     - (c) Religious Scholars
     - (d) Deliverance Ministers
     - (e) Summary

CHAPTER 9. FAILURES

1. False Failures
2. The Sufferer
3. The Minister
   - (i) Lack of Determination
   - (ii) Lack of Discernment
   - (iii) Lack of Authority
   - (iv) Lack of Power

CHAPTER 10. CONCLUSIONS

1. The Purpose of the Deliverance Ministry
   - (i) Evidence of the Kingdom or Rule of God
   - (ii) Preparation of the Bride
   - (iii) In answer to our Prayers
   - (iv) To set the captives free

BOOK 4 "DISCERNING HUMAN NATURE"
TO BE RE-STRUCTURED

TRADE AND MINISTRY ENQUIRIES

Trade enquiries to:

U.S.A.
Impact Books Inc.
137 W. Jefferson
Kirkwood
Missouri 63122
U.S.A.
Tel. (314) 822-3309
Fax (314) 822-3325

PHILIPPINES
Peter & Susan Magee
P.O. Box 178
Cagayan de Oro City 9000
PHILIPPINESS

AFRICA
SJBS Outreach Inc.
P.O. Box 4953 Oshodi
Lagos
NIGERIA

MALAYSIA
Arise Shine Centre
Lot 8946 Jalan Foochow No. 2
93300 Kuching, Sarawak
MALAYSIA
Tel. (82) – 481168,
Fax (82) 244098

UNITED KINGDOM

Diasozo Trust
90 St. Mary's Rd,
Market Harborough
Leics LE 16 7DX
ENGLAND
Tel. (0858)434168
Fax (0858) 433385

New Wine Ministries
Unit 22, Arun Business Park
Shripney Road, Bognor Regis
West Sussex PO 22, 9SX
ENGLAND
Tel. 0243 867227
Fax 0243 867292

AUSTRALIA. Trade and Ministry enquires to:
Full Salvation Fellowship Ltd.
P.O.Box 1020
Crows Nest, 2065
AUSTRALIA
Tel. (02) 436 3657
Fax (02) 906 2663

OTHER PUBLICATIONS

This book is the Seventh publication by FULL SALVATION FELLOWSHIP LTD designed to assist the people of God in their preparation for the drama of the End Time, which we believe has already begun on God's calendar.

The others published are:

"Guidance for Those Receiving Deliverance"

"The Re-incarnation Deception"

"Man, Woman, HEADCOVERING and Lady Pastor-Teachers"

"Christian Authority and Power"

"Surviving the Distress of Nations"

"End-Time Deliverance"

"Your Full Salvation"

Christian Deliverance Book 1 - "Make Yourselves Ready"

Christian Deliverance Book 3 - "Walking in Victory"

Others in the process of production and to be published soon are:

Christian Deliverance Book 4 -"Discerning Human Nature"

"Sex, Demons and Morality"

"Musical Hypnosis"

"The Stigmata of Jesus"

Also "A fresh Look" series on widely debated subjects, such as:

"Baptism - Water and Spirit"

"Fullness and Tongues"

* * * * *

"Your books have been a real blessing. As a minister of the Gospel ... I know that this is what is needed, and by God's grace will begin to minister to others ..."

Alan K. Taylor
Kent, **England.**

"Engaging the Enemy'... exposes principles of warfare in the Old Testament that will help those who are seeking to be a mighty man of valour .. expressed in concise words that helps the reader to enter the conflict, **as though he were present when the enemy is engaged."**

Pastor Kevin S. Wedrat
A.O.G. Church
Goondiwindi, QLD. **Australia.**

.... I happened to see one of your books on Christian Deliverance - (Book 2 - How to Engage the Enemy"). It was very much helpful for me. **It gave me new insights** into many fields, especially continuous deliverance.

Cheriyan Thomas
Kundara, **South India.**

"As I'm reading the book of 'Christian Deliverance', **I'm really touched and encouraged and inspired** to continue what the Lord has been doing to my life. Please send me the complete series ..."

Bro. Bing Gadian
Jesus For All Ministries
Mindanao, **Philippines**.

It is certainly **a book for the serious ministry student.** One could say that it extends the groundwork laid by writers such as **Frank and Ida Mae Hammond** and **Kenneth E. Hagin,** and ranks an easy-to-reach place on your shelf right alongside **Bill Subritzky. 'Engaging the Enemy' makes a very valuable and scholarly contribution** to a needy and much maligned area of teaching.

'Engaging the Enemy' - Book 2 in the 'Christian Deliverance' series.
Reviewed by Steve Bewlay
Sydney, **Australia.**